TIME

TIDDY ROWAN

Your Journey to a Slower, Richer,
More Fulfilling Way of Life

piatkus

PIATKUS

First published in Great Britain in 2019 by Piatkus

1 3 5 7 9 10 8 6 4 2

A CIP catalogue record for this book is available from the British Library.

ISBN 978-0-349-42102-5

Printed and bound in Great Britain by Clays Ltd, Elcograf S.p.A.

Papers used by Piatkus are from well-managed forests
and other responsible sources.

Piatkus
An imprint of
Little, Brown Book Group
Carmelite House
50 Victoria Embankment
London EC4Y 0DZ

An Hachette UK Company
www.hachette.co.uk

www.littlebrown.co.uk

For Holly

'To say "I don't have time", is like saying:
"I don't want to."'

LAO TZU

INTRODUCTION

I have been fascinated by the subject of time, even as a child trying to grasp the illusion of it. Later in life I had the realisation that our 24-hour clock represents a daily currency – a currency that is the most vital asset we have. I set off on a path to see how I could manage to spend my time better, more wisely and happier.

In order to increase my appreciation for this vital asset I wanted to get to know the subject better, and I began looking into other aspects of time: when it began, if indeed it ever did begin, or whether it always existed, the beginnings of time-making equipment, and time as quantified in physics and science. I widened my appreciation by looking closely at time in its most unadulterated form, in nature: in the annual and repet-itive budding and flowering, the rotation of planets and stars on a cyclical basis, the rising and falling of the tides and the very nature of us humans and our own, natural circadian rhythms.

My interest grew larger by the day; the more I read,

the more there was to know. In undertaking to write about the subject I had a choice: to research a book on time which would or could take me the rest of my life, or to try to channel some of the aspects of time that I have learned so far and that have helped me to shape a richer, slower life. I have chosen the latter.

The thread that binds the topics in this book is the constant return to the human dimension within time and dealing with the dichotomy we encounter when living between our own natural rhythms and the superimposed clock of human-made time. The book is intended to help serve as a reminder of the fleetingness of time, and the importance of living in the present, with awareness, as much as possible.

The one thing that is shared by all humanity is time, irrespective of wealth, health, race or creed; and one of the things that make each one of us individual is how we choose to spend it. Of all the assets we have, time is the most vital. Without it we have nothing. Even if fortune and good health elude us, if we still have time, we have hope. When we have no more time, we have, literally, no more life.

It is all too easy to disregard its importance. Isn't it time we took back control over how we spend it, while we still can?

Tiddy Rowan
November 2019

WHAT IS TIME?

The *Concise Oxford Dictionary* definition of time fills two columns, and it is about the same in the *Chambers Twentieth Century Dictionary*. In Roget's *Thesaurus* 59 timepieces are listed — and that's without all the primitive methods of time-keeping, which have their own names.

If I had to choose one from the *Concise Oxford Dictionary* it would be: 'The indefinite continued progress of existence and events in the past, present, and future regarded as a whole.' From *Chambers* it would be: 'moment at which, or stretch of duration in which, things happen'.

I'm not about to challenge the revered compilers and editors of these lexicons, but I'm not sure that either of these vocabulary entries states what time actually is.

Time doesn't mind whether something happens in it or not, which refutes the *Chambers'* definition. Similarly, in the *Concise Oxford*, although we might relate time to the progress of our existence, time existed and will continue to exist in itself without our individual existence. You see what we're up against in trying to get to the very crux of time itself?

If humankind invented a word to describe 'time' and proceeded to apply a mathematical construction to this invention, then, equally, humankind has fallen victim to its own invention. It can't unknow what it has long since created.

The choice confronting us all is whether to proceed with the man-made contrivance, and therefore continue to be caught in its intricate web, or somehow to find a way out. Guided by nature's own clock of the Sun and the Moon, and our own natural circadian rhythm, we can, to a greater degree, escape the total imposition of the artificial time machine and take back our own mastery of days and nights.

If we could escape human-made time, wouldn't society as we know it fall apart? If everyone followed their own clock, wouldn't that result in chaos? You might well ask: isn't it too late to turn the 'clocks' back? But no, society would not fall apart – it would provide a different society; it would not create chaos, because the simple truth is that not everyone is going to alter their clocks completely.

We are never going to switch to *only* following our own natural time frame if we live in a societal framework, but we can adapt to a time frame that follows a more natural course.

No one is suggesting returning to the Stone Age,

but I'm also suggesting not being carried along on this ever-speeding conveyor belt into an increasingly spiritless future governed by the dinning of the digital tick – without at least questioning it or inspecting it.

We do have choices.

Let's inspect the nature of time so that we can make those informed choices.

IN THE BEGINNING . . . BANG!

Wait a minute – what beginning? It seems to be generally accepted that the universe – and with it time and space – was created, or came about, at a finite moment in the past, conforming to the Big Bang theory. But let's not forget that it is only a *theory*. Even the neurophysicist and scientist Stephen Hawking reminded us in his book, *A Brief History of Time*, that 'any physical theory is always provisional, in the sense that it is only a hypothesis: you can never prove it'.

Nothing is proven. If theoretical physicists, scientists and philosophers mostly concur that all theories on the beginning (and therefore the end) of time are hypothetical, it leaves me (questionably and with some gusto, and even temerity) at liberty to speculate or posit that there *was* no beginning.

If the entire universe suddenly *did* expand out of an infinitely hot, infinitely dense singularity some 13.8 billion years ago with the Big Bang, there would, surely, have had to be a space and therefore a time to pre-exist that singularity's existence. In other words, whenever the universe began, time itself had to already have existed for it to be created into. There are no proven theories, and so we're free to kick around our own theories and opinions.

'Who cares about the half a second after the big bang; what about the half a second before?'

FAY WELDON

INFINITY

As a child, do you remember standing under the enormity of the night sky lit up by millions of bright twinkling stars and, for the first time, truly wondering at it? You would pinch yourself trying to imagine that the sky had no end, trying to come to grips with the notion of infinity – infinity in space and time. Some of that magic never entirely leaves us, and at times we can find ourselves under the same night sky and feel something of that wonderment and the sheer giddiness of infinity's reality. That's the feeling I'd like to evoke as we travel through, and around, time itself.

A FEW THOUGHTS ON THE ORIGIN OF TIME

Turtles all the way down An Eastern guru affirms that the Earth is supported on the back of a tiger. When asked what supports the tiger, he says it stands upon an elephant; and when asked what supports the elephant he says it is a giant turtle. When asked, finally, what supports the giant turtle, he is briefly taken aback, but quickly replies, 'Ah, after that it is turtles all the way down.'

The philosopher Bertrand Russell famously used a version of this fable in a lecture on the subject of time to illustrate the confoundedness of the subject.

Ancient Greece The early Greek philosophers generally believed that the universe (and therefore time itself) was infinite with no beginning and no end. In the fifth century BCE, the Sophist philosopher Antiphon asserted that time is not a reality but a concept or a measure. Also in the fifth century BC, Parmenides saw time (as well as motion and many other everyday things that we take for granted) as nothing more than an illusion, because, he argued, all change is impossible and illusory. (Time as an illusion is also a common theme in Buddhist thought). Parmenides, then, believed that reality was limited to what exists in the here and now, and the past and future are unreal and imaginary. His near contemporary Heraclitus, on the other hand, firmly believed that the flow of time is real and the very essence of reality.

Back(s) to the future In the afterword of *Zen and the Art of Motorcycle Maintenance*, Robert Pirsig draws our attention to a view held by the Ancient Greeks on their notion of time. They saw themselves as backing into the future, facing the past as it receded.

In many ways this perspective makes sense, since all we know is the past and the present. It makes little sense facing into future time, since it is completely unknown – like walking forward into a thick fog. We become obsessed by this non-existent future with a remarkable degree of confidence that it will unfold according to our human brain's directions.

By facing the past with a clear view, being informed by it to guide us through present time, and our backs against the tide of oncoming time, we are better positioned to be less obsessed by future time and able to concentrate more fully on the present.

HUMANKIND'S FIRST TIME-KEEPING DEVICES

Quite apart from any scientific theories and discoveries regarding time itself, humankind has been measuring time in order to keep track of our daily lives.

Since humankind emerged on the planet, time-keeping devices became an integral part of our lives.

Deep time and the ancient Maya

The day, or *k'in*, was the most important aspect of Maya time: all Maya counts come down to the passing of the days. *K'in* also means 'sun', which is related to the Indo-European root *dyeu* for our 'day', which means 'to shine'. As far as we know, there was no word in the ancient Mayan languages for 'time' but the Maya, like us, kept detailed track of the passing of the days going back millennia. (Maya civilisation existed in what archaeologists term the Preclassic Period 1800BC to AD250.)

The Maya had, and indeed still have, named days that were more or less conceptually equivalent to our week. There were differences. Their week, or *tzolkin*, count had 13 numbers, whereas our week uses seven numbers. The Maya had 20 named days in the *tzolkin*, whereas we have only seven named days: Sunday through Saturday. Another difference is that day one of our week is always Sunday, whereas in the Maya week, the numbers one to 13 were matched with the 20 named days, which meant that their weekly cycle was 260 days rather than just seven. This seems complicated, but in fact it is easy for people to remember and was probably how most people kept track of time.

Like us, the Maya had months which made up a count called *haab*, somewhat like our year. There were 18 named months (for example, *Pop*, *Yaxkin*) of 20 days each, with a short month of five days (called *Wayeb*) tacked on at the end of the 18-month cycle. This gave the Maya a count of 365 days, which approximates our solar year. The Maya, however, made no attempt, as we do, to have the start of their 'yearly' cycle always begin on day one of the same named month; in our case the first of January. For our year to do this we have to have months of different lengths, and we have to manipulate the counts, as we do with February. The Maya months were always 20 days with the five-day month at the cycle's end, and this simply meant that their annual cycles started with different days of different months. In a way this is like our weeks – we don't try to make the first day of the year fall on a Sunday, for example. It can fall on any of the named days of the week.

These weekly and monthly cycles kept track of the passing of the days, but the distinctiveness of Maya time-keeping is that, like us, the Maya counted absolute time based on the date of a crucially important event. We do not know the significance of the Maya starting date, but we do know that it is equivalent in our calendar to 13 August, 3114BC. Thus, Maya sky-watchers were keeping accurate track of time when Europeans were transitioning from the Neolithic to the Bronze Age! There are carved monuments that count cycles of days that go back long before 3114BC, which hints that the 3114 BC event did not, strictly speaking, represent the creation of the Maya world, as many Mayanists argue. This would mean that, remarkably, long before Charles Darwin and James Hutton, the Maya had a concept of deep time.

DR ELIZABETH GRAHAM,
Professor of mesoamerican archaeology, University College London institute of archaeology

THE BEGINNING OF TIME-KEEPING?
THE WORLD'S OLDEST 'CALENDAR' DISCOVERED

British archaeology experts have discovered what they believe to be the world's oldest 'calendar', created by hunter-gatherer societies and dating back to around 8,000 BC.

The Mesolithic monument was originally excavated in Aberdeenshire, Scotland, by the National Trust for Scotland in 2004. New analysis by a team led by the University of Birmingham, published on 15 July 2013 in the journal *Internet Archaeology*, sheds remarkable new light on the luni–solar device, which pre-dates the first formal time-measuring devices known to human-kind, found in the Near East, by nearly 5,000 years.

The capacity to measure time is among the most important of human achievements and the issue of when time was 'created' by humankind is critical in understanding how society has developed.

Until the 21st century, the first formal calendars appear to have been created in Mesopotamia *c.*5,000 years ago. But a monument created by hunter-gatherers in Aberdeenshire nearly 10,000 years ago, appears to mimic the phases of the Moon in order to track lunar months over the course of a year.

The site, at Warren Field, Crathes, also aligns on the midwinter sunrise, providing an annual astronomic correction in order to maintain the link between the passage of time, indicated by the Moon, the asynchronous solar year and the associated seasons.

Project leader Vince Gaffney, professor of landscape archaeology at the University of Bradford, comments: 'The evidence suggests that hunter-gatherer societies in Scotland had both the need and sophistication to track time across the years, to correct for seasonal drift of the lunar year and that this occurred nearly 5,000 years before the first formal calendars known in the Near East. In doing so, this illustrates a step towards the formal construction of time and therefore history itself.'

DRAWN TO THE MOON

Professor Vince Gaffney got me thinking, as did the research made in 1920 on early time-reckoning. The Moon that we all look at was the guiding inspiration for time-telling (and to a degree the position of the stars, too) for earliest human-kind all over the globe. And not just in one place – they all shared the same Moon: Native Americans, Mesopotamians, Aboriginal people and primitive tribes, and it was gradually shared, too, by later civilisations. Subsequently, we had Julius Caesar's calendar and then Pope Gregory's (from which we take our own time-telling).

All this was to do with the Moon. It turns out that the calendar couldn't really be based around the Sun because the Earth, and with it the Moon, is constantly changing its position, giving us a relative reading, or reckoning, against the Sun's central position.

Tonight we see the same Moon that earliest human-kind reckoned with. How wonderful is that? And so our relationship with time is linked with the Moon whether or not we are aware of it – it's all lunar. The clock might be a development of man's early time-keeping device, but it all starts with the Moon.

If there were a solar storm that wiped out all our watches and clocks, we would still have the Moon by which to mark our days, our months and our seasons.

In 1859, an invisible wave crashed into the Earth, named the Carrington Event after the scientist, Richard Carrington, who recorded it. It was the largest solar storm ever recorded. If it happened today, it would jeopardise global tele-communications, and knock out orbiting satellites and with them GPS, mobile-phone reception and power grids. The global aircraft fleet would have to coordinate an unprecedented mass grounding without satellite guidance. Unguarded electronic infrastructure could fail outright. With it, our notion of a centrally useful, human-made time would need to undergo recalibration.

'And hand in hand, on the edge
of the sand,
They danced by the light of the moon.'

'The Owl and the Pussycat',
EDWARD LEAR

PRIMITIVE TIME-KEEPING

I like the simplicity in the tradition of the early inhabitants of the New Hebrides (and perhaps the tradition continues among their tribal population) of pointing to where the Sun would be in the sky to indicate the time of, for example, a proposed meeting. Australian Aborigines and other tribes, globally, naturally point to the Sun and say, 'When the Sun stands there' to tell the time.

The Javanese were known to use the shadows of the Sun; for example, they would pace out the number of feet to indicate the length of the shadow and therefore the 'time' of day. A traveller set out on a journey or arrived at the end of it when his shadow was 'so many feet long'.

The Cross River native people of Obubura Hill District in Southern Nigeria had in most of their houses a plant about 50cm high with violet-white flowers by which to tell the time. The flowers gradually open at sunrise, by noon they are wide open, and they gradually close again between noon and sunset.

Some time-telling devices undoubtedly work better

in the tropics where the Sun consistently stands high throughout the year. Anyone interested in exploring these and many more early time-reckonings might enjoy *Primitive Time-Reckoning* by Martin Nilsson published in 1920.

No Native American tribe had a true calendar: a single integrated system of denoting days and longer periods of time. Usually, intervals of time were counted independently of one another.

The day was a basic unit recognised by all tribes, but there is no record of names for days. A common device for keeping track of days was a bundle of sticks of known number, from which one was extracted for every day that passed, until the bundle was exhausted. Longer periods of time were usually counted by moons, which began with the New Moon or the conjunction of the Sun and Moon.

Years were divided into four seasons, occasionally five, and, when counted, were usually designated by one of the seasons; for example, a North American Indian might say that a certain event had happened ten winters ago.

The naming of moons is perhaps the first step in transforming them into months. The Zuni Indians of New Mexico named the first six moons of the year, referring to the remainder by colour designations associated with the four cardinal (horizontal) directions, and the zenith and the nadir.

Only a few Indian tribes attempted a more precise correlation of moons and years.

American Indians have a litany of wonderful such names. Some of my favourites are:

Full Wolf Moon (January)
The Little Frog Moon (March)
Strawberry Moon (June)
The Moon of the Wild Rice (September)
Full Buck Moon (July)

Naming of the moons was not limited to North America, it occurred in tribal cultures across the world. In cultures where people lived a more time-natural life, the Moon itself was specifically named as an indicator of the month or the season. Some were less lyrical than others; for example, the Finnish named their calendars after what happens to their reindeer, including the arduous-sounding month 'When the Reindeers' Parasites Emerge'!

'When I began living and working in Indian country [this refers to American Indian], I learned the origin of the phrase "Indian time". I came to understand that traditionally Indian people were very good students of nature. They studied the seasons and the animals to learn how to live well in their environments. Given this, they learned that it's important to be patient and to act when circumstances were "ripe" rather than to try to force things to happen when circumstances did not support them. I have come to understand it's a Western idea that we can control most circumstances and that we should run our lives by the clock and the calendar. It makes more sense to plant crops when the weather is right than when the calendar says it is time.'

KELLY GIBSON

A SIGNIFICANT SHIFT IN TIME-TELLING

When visiting rural parts of the world, we are reminded of the vital role that the Sun and the Moon continue to play in agrarian societies. But with increased urbanisation, and the onset of the Industrial Revolution in the West, an agricultural-based life with its cycles of natural time was phased out. In its stead came a rush of new developments in modern industry, engineering, commerce, travel, communication and government.

Central to this need was a way of getting workers to these factories and energy plants, so railway networks were built, and they flourished.

Very soon a problem presented itself: a train timetable that the whole population could work to. Until then, a collective need for sharing time was limited to a small radius of people, in a village or a town, to call worshippers to church or the workers to the field, usually by the ringing of the church bells because the church clock was the central timekeeper. (There is a wonderful old church clock in the Provençal town of Lorgues that still rings out the time of day twice at each clock hour. This is a habit left over from a time before everyone had a clock or a watch. If the workers or worshippers didn't hear the full chimes on the first ring they knew they could count the chimes again on the second ring.)

With towns being linked by train networks and thus broadening the radius of communities, it became necessary to compile a train timetable that the whole population could work to. The problem was that before Greenwich Mean Time was invented, there were disparities between clock times in towns further apart from each other; for example, when it was midday in London, Paddington, it might have been 12.30 in the south-west of the country, Penzance.

At each station hung a large station clock, by which travellers would adjust the time on their pocket watches accordingly. This caused havoc when compilers of train timetables went about their compiling, since there was no one central time to adhere to. In 1847 the heads of British train companies agreed that all timetables would be aligned to Greenwich Observatory time. Other companies and institutions followed suit and, in 1880, Britain collectively adhered to a national artificially devised time and standardised clocks in a break away from traditional sunrise/sunset-led time.

A new dawn had broken. And from that time on, an international network of timetables developed, not only for the railways but also for airlines, radio, television and other communication networks.

'Time is money.'

Advice to Young Tradesmen,
BENJAMIN FRANKLIN (1748)

If money really is time – to invert the Benjamin Franklin quote – then take Warren Buffet's investment advice and apply it to your time stock:

'Make a list of your twenty-five top goals then go through it and circle the top five and act on those. They will be the [time] investments you really believe in.'

PIP, PIP, PIP!

A tradition among newscasters on radio and television is to still announce – even before world headlines – the time. This is usually with great solemnity by pips, or in the case of the UK by the chimes of Big Ben. This gives the obedient population a chance to make sure that their watches are correct should they have slipped by as much as a minute. Of course, we now have our smartphones, which are not only calibrated to give us the *exact* time, but they are also programmed to take in the putting forward and putting back of clocks twice a year to adjust for summer daylight hours.

Tide tables are still published that continue to cite the differences between coastal time around the country. I like the nod here to a more primitive time-keeping, incapable of being updated or centralised.

WHAT TIME IS IT IN . . .?

In an archaic-sounding way, we might still ask each other on the phone across countries and time lines, 'What time is it with you?' Or, 'What time is it there?'

We have a return to published times in the shape of apps that tell us what time it is in these different countries and what the time difference is between us.

Here's a thought: will there come a time when the world is governed by a centralised, common time?

We might ask, 'Are we behind California or ahead of it?' and then become momentarily mystified as to what happens to the lost or gained hours when we travel between different continents.

TORN IN TIME

I believe that one of our innermost instinctual dilemmas is that of being *torn between two types of time*:

1. We are rooted in natural time, because we are natural animals: our very heart beats in time with the Earth's.

And yet ...

2. We are bound by time in an artificial way, by clocks devised by man for enterprise, business, work schedules, travel, and so on.

Perhaps we still have a natural response to *real* time, even more than we are aware of as we go about our lives dictated by atomic clocks tuned to fractions of a second of artificial time.

Wearing a watch binds us almost literally to artificial time. Whenever we look at it, it reinforces our tie to human-made time.

We can at least recognise this divergence, and

through that recognition make the choice not to wear watches all the time (it is somehow more of an action to look up the time on our phones than it is to glance at a watch). When we need to know the time, it will be there – everywhere. And we only really need to know the time when we have a plane or a train to catch, a meeting to attend, a child's birthday party to get to, a dentist appointment, and so on. But in between these siren calls of society we can glide effortlessly into our natural time frame, so that there is less inner disparity.

Time is actually speeding up (or collapsing)

For thousands of years, the Schumann resonance, or pulse (heartbeat), of Earth has been 7.83 cycles per second. The military have used this as a very reliable reference, apparently; however, since 1980 this resonance has been slowly rising. Some scientists believe that it is rising faster than we can measure it, because it is constantly rising while it is being measured. All objects have a natural frequency at which they vibrate. The Earth is understood to vibrate between 3 and 60Hz, and the human body at between 2 and 10Hz. Our bodies, including our brain waves and possibly even our states of consciousnesses, are correlated to the Earth's frequencies; for example, the resonant frequency of the human wrist is about 2Hz for large oscillations but rises to approximately 10Hz for small ones. The Schumann resonance is a good place to start for further understanding in this area.

This might explain why we feel that time is

going faster and faster – how come it's already your birthday again? – because in fact it really is speeding up, and your birthday really does come around quicker.

'I never follow the clock: hours were made for man, not man for hours.'

Gargantua,
FRANÇOIS RABELAIS

ESCAPE FROM TIME

The more often we have personal experiences of being 'outside of time', in a realm other than the artificial clock, the more we can balance one with the other.

The physicist Ernest Barnes in his 1929 Gifford Lectures eloquently described this combination of timelessness and clarity.

> 'I remember that I was going to a stretch of shingle to which few people who stayed in the village seldom went. Suddenly the noise of the insects was hushed. Time seemed to stop. A sense of infinite power and peace came upon me. I can best liken the combination of timelessness with amazing fullness of existence to the feeling one gets in watching the unmoving surface of a deep, strongly flowing river. Nothing happened: yet existence was completely full. All was clear.'

Barnes captures the fleeting glimpses we have of this kind. Be on the lookout for such moments – captured with the awareness of a dragonfly on the water.

SLOWING DOWN

Global news, media and social pressure leads to a compulsion to fall in line, be competitive, outpace others, win imaginary races and generally live outside our own natural inclinations in the pursuit of unrealistic goals. As a result, people complain about being time-poor, being under pressure, having time slip away from them or being constantly harried by the past and concerned about the future; their constant refrain: 'I haven't got time!'

There is, though, in the midst of all this, a growing sense that the appetite of the personal pendulum is beginning to swing away from globalisation and back towards our own world, our community, our circle, friends and family – and ultimately towards finding our own inner rhythm again amid the turbulence of the bigger world.

This is evidenced by the appeal that the Slow Food movement had at its inception. Spearheaded by Carlo Petrini in Rome in 1986 and a small group of friends in protest at McDonald's opening its franchise in the historic Piazza de Spagna, the movement soon grew in popularity – in favour of a return to slower cooking and slower eating. The movement grew globally and appealed to those wanting slower living altogether, to slow the tide of fast waves in every area of our lives.

We need a better relationship with time – time is on our side if we choose it to be. And, by knowing it better, and understanding it better, we can make it our servant, not our master – or, best of all, our friend.

'We live in time – it holds us and moulds us – but I never felt I understood it very well. And I'm not referring to theories about how it bends and doubles back, or may exist elsewhere in parallel versions. No, I mean ordinary, everyday time, which clocks and watches assure us passes regularly: tick-tock, click-clock. Is there anything more plausible than a second hand? And yet it takes only the smallest pleasure or pain to teach us time's malleability. Some emotions speed it up, others slow it down; occasionally, it seems to go missing – until the eventual point when it really does go missing, never to return.'

The Sense of an Ending,
JULIAN BARNES

We are all granted a share in time, in this abstruse quality that has been around for an eternity (or at least billions of years, depending on your viewpoint). There is enough time for everyone, however much the population grows, and that, even better, we each have a daily supply of it for the duration of our life span.

We then home in on the only very real moment in all this vast abstract concept of time, the moment we are in, which makes it so illusory, so hard to grasp. But the simplicity, out of all the complex theories on the subject, is exactly that: to grasp the moment in time that we're in. Which, since you are reading these words, is precisely now!

It seems there is a design function in human evolution in that we have a fear of reaching the end of our time. When we are children the idea of life ending is so far-fetched, so far into some hazy future that we do not fear it. But at some point, we develop this fear. Not in the way prey fears its predator, but the simple fear of having no more time. At some point in our lives though, much later, we become reconciled to the idea. Many people who are very old feel their time has come and gone and they are ready to move on. What we need to do is deal with the underlying fear that exists somewhere between the two extremes of our lives.

Statistics that concentrate the mind

At the age of 30 a healthy person can look forward to perhaps another 60 years on this planet. That is 720 months, a mere 3,120 weeks, an hourly allowance of 525,000, a total currency of 31,500,000 minutes. Tick-tock. And if you should be older and reading this – say 60 years old – that total allowance suddenly dwindles to perhaps only another mere 11,000 days, which equals roughly 264,000 hours of time left on this planet.

VALUE OUR TIME

This is not meant to depress you in any way, but on the contrary to act as a siren call to us all to value each of those days and hours – moments in time.

This brings us to our present senses and the knowledge of how much time we have to spend on a daily basis, and yet the paradox is that our time is diminishing – daily. Perhaps the best we can do is cultivate awareness, sharpen our senses, value our time more. Maybe we need to change our relationship radically with time. It is different for everyone, and it is up to us, individually, to make that assessment and fine-tuning. It is not a chore, it is not a question of we should do this, it is not a question of having to carve out time for awareness. It is something to come to either gradually or in an instant, depending on our already open receptivity to the idea that changes will be positive, enlightening, joyful.

Imagine that it was only now, at this moment of reading, that you were bestowed with an amazing life-long benefaction that would last for the rest of your life: a daily allowance of an exquisite gift. That, to make it easier for you to grasp, this asset would be made up of

24 manageable units – a currency that you could use or dispense however you like and, what's more, that it would be like a repeat prescription that you would have ready and waiting for you each and every day. Oh, and it's free!

The only caveat is that you cannot get back the time units already spent, and we cannot know how many days of them are ahead of us.

'Since time is the one immaterial object
which we cannot influence – neither speed
up nor slow down, add to nor diminish – it
is an imponderably valuable gift.'

Wouldn't Take Nothing
For My Journey Now,
MAYA ANGELOU

MAKE FRIENDS WITH TIME

By now, perhaps, we have begun to make friends with time in its broadest sense. Only by getting to know about a person, or in this case subject, with whom we have a relationship, can we gain a depth of understanding and value. The more we make friends with time the less we will be controlled by it.

Henry David Thoreau in his seminal book, *Walden: Life In the Woods*, tells the story of an artist who sets out to make a staff – a wooden stick. The artist comes to the observation that in an imperfect work, time is an ingredient, 'but into a perfect work, time does not enter ... As he made no compromise with Time, Time kept out of his way and only sighed at a distance because it could not overcome him.'

'There exists, therefore, for the individual, an I-time, or subjective time. This in itself is not measurable.'

ALBERT EINSTEIN

The more that social data is continually compiled from our social media activity into algorithms that track our preferences, our habits, tastes and personal lifestyles, the more we are being dictated to and directed subversively into doing things with our time that are not necessarily our primary choices.

A good tip that I picked up doing research for this book was to put my phone on to airplane mode. It prevents being constantly at its beck and beep – you look to see what beeped, then have a roam around checking emails, news updates, WhatsApps, and so on, and find that 20 minutes have gone by. On airplane mode you have to make that extra effort to check in, and it makes you time-richer.

'Old friends pass away, new friends appear. It is just like the days. An old day passes, a new day arrives. The important thing is to make it meaningful: a meaningful friend – or a meaningful day.'

DALAI LAMA

Philosophers and sages alike have long suggested that impermanence or the passage of time is at the root of our suffering. The philosopher Hans Reichenbach, on the matter in his book, *The Direction of Time*, suggested that it might have been in order to escape from this anxiety that the Greek philosopher Parmenides denied time's existence.

Georg Wilhelm Friedrich Hegel spoke of the moment in which the spirit transcends temporality. He suggested that it might be because of this that we have imagined the existence of 'eternity'– a world outside time that we imagine inhabited by gods, a god or immortal souls in order to give hope to the otherwise finality of physical immortality.

Perhaps, by getting to know time better, understanding it from our *own* perspective, and removing it from the category of mystery in our minds, it will give us back a more natural tempo.

PLAYTIME

We are mostly self-taught in how to use our time. Children at play or left to follow their own direction and inclinations naturally echo their own rhythms and paces, whether it's following a snail trail, reading under a tree somewhere or rounding up other children to play an energetic game of tag. Children set off into worlds of their own; discovering and shaping them for the first time. This private, personal freedom to explore is priceless.

They have, to a certain extent, an affinity for the outdoors – where their primeval instincts can set about building a den, a shelter, a house. The beach offers driftwood to build their boat, or caves for more houses. Forests and woods give them trees and tree houses – nests that take their inspiration from the eagles and prehistoric birds of their imagination.

As children get older, this ability to follow their own timing in finishing homework, a project or essay that requires a deadline, will eventually give them their own motivation and scheduling. But beyond that, the freedom of time that parents can give a child throughout their childhood allows them to find their *thing*, the *thing* that grows within them and becomes central to their life's exploration, the root of a passion, a talent, a direction that they might otherwise never find in life or only later with a concerted effort to do so.

Take a moment to identify what that 'thing' is that makes you happy and feel in tune with life itself. Reflect on your own childhood and bring to mind how you spent your time and what made you happy and fulfilled for hours on end.

'We don't stop playing because we grow old; we grow old because we stop playing.'

GEORGE BERNARD SHAW

IN THIS MOMENT...

> And in this moment ...
>> And in this moment ...

This is a good mantra to repeat slowly during meditation to help us to stay in the present moment, with awareness. The phrase can be said in its simplicity or added to, depending on what we are feeling on that particular day.

> In this moment I do not feel fear,
> In this moment I am not anxious,
> In this moment I feel well,
> In this moment I have courage.

MIND-TIME

Do you find yourself constantly reverting to a stream of jumbled thoughts when your mind is left to its own devices? Either you're happy with that or, if not, is there room for tidying up those thoughts? When you find yourself free-associating in random, stray thoughts that don't add up to anything, try to pull them back into shape and spend mind-time editing them, corralling those thoughts as though tidying an untidy desk or house. There are different rooms in the mind for different topics.

When you are time-rich, you can go to one of the 'rooms' to reflect on a particular topic: choose a topic to think about. Your mind-time will be clearer and work more efficiently.

'What then is time? If no one asks me, I know what it is.

If I wish to explain it to him who asks, I do not know.'

SAINT AUGUSTINE

MAKE TIME TO PROGRAM OUR
INNER MINDSET

We need to allow time for the inner workings of our inherently lucid minds to perform their role of managing our decisions, plans and lives to the utmost.

Because our 'essence' (the subconscious, inner voice, or whatever we like to call it) is beyond reach of the rational mind, it makes sense to recognise that we need to suspend our everyday thinking in order to hear those inner workings. It's like feeding information about your ambitions, hopes, expectations or plans into a very sophisticated computer, and then, with the aid of algorithms, the best scenario, understanding or advice is then presented to you.

A lot of the discontent, anxiety and stress we feel in many aspects of our hectic lives are due to a lack of proper understanding, appreciation and use of time. We need to find ways to rediscover our true instincts, direction, priorities, rhythm and real needs in life.

Through awareness of time and how we spend it, and a simple recalibration, we can continue on our journey of life with renewed joy, confidence and wisdom – and an appreciation of our valuable time.

We have to want to make those changes, which might range from one or two simple adjustments to a total life overhaul.

CLEAR YOUR CLUTTER

Firstly, we have to clear the clutter, in the same way we would in the kitchen if we were going to prepare a meal. Whether a simple meal or a banquet, both require us first of all to clear space on the surfaces, do any washing up and lay out our ingredients. We will work better this way, undistracted by peripheral clutter. In fact, the better we prepare the space, the better the meal will be. We all know the difference when eating a meal that has been provided for us which has been prepared in this way: with pleasure, care and generosity.

So it is when we want to *clear our minds of clutter*, using meditation of some sort (sitting, walking, hiking, or whatever it is that we can do with the least distraction in order to allow our deeper instincts and guidance to come to the fore). Sitting in a quiet room is in many ways the best, since there are no external interferences; however, it's true that a different form of mind clearing comes about when we are surrounded by nature or preoccupied with our physical safety: when rock climbing, sailing, hiking or skiing.

The simple purpose of meditation is really to give ourselves a mental breather, to stop the rush of time going past us unnoticed, to pause between the busy agenda we set ourselves or allow ourselves to fall into – that constant harried hurrying. In other words, deck clearing.

With our minds cleared of clutter on a regular basis through a state of meditation, we can begin to practise awareness. Being aware of being aware. Focusing on awareness itself (be it 10, 15, 20 minutes or more). We could take one simple phrase or idea to guide us. Let's take the idea that we want to *improve our awareness* and strengthen that muscle of attention.

Straight away, after only a few seconds, our minds start wandering into other thoughts, one leading on to another like connected carriages in a runaway train. This is already a good place to start practising our awareness in being aware that these random thoughts are coming in uninvited, by stepping back and watching the thoughts as though they were happening independently of us. By doing this we are being aware. Let them go.

Come back to the centre where it is calm and quiet.

Be aware of this and the gentle pleasure that comes from dwelling there.

By becoming more adept at finding these quieter pools, these thoughts will gradually join together to give longer periods where you realise that you truly *are* living in this awareness, in this moment. This is not in a narrow intellectual way but in everyday life, in the true freedom that comes about by living consciously – living an authentic life.

There is no knowing what will come to you. It depends on your state of mind and how and when you are able to access this idea of awareness, consciously. But you will know what freedom, clarity, joy, calmness and unexpected bursts of happiness are, and you will be stronger and better able to deal with pain and loss, seeing that, too, with awareness, and knowing it changes with every passing moment.

There are opportunities throughout the day when we have a few moments – waiting for the kettle to boil or making a cup of tea or coffee, preparing a packed lunch, waiting in a queue – when we can benefit from a brief meditation exercise.

Stop the thoughts in order to focus on the breathing. Three or five slower breaths in then out, just concentrating on the breath. It's extraordinary how, after a while, it's as though the thoughts are tamed. They come to a natural halt when focusing solely on the breathing.

After a period of meditation (or conscious thought displacement through physical activity) you will continue to go about your day but you will gradually become more and more aware of that calm centre to return to. Your senses will sharpen and you will naturally become more aware of what you are doing in the eternal present. In short, you will find yourself paying attention naturally, promoting a more valuable and productive life.

Part of clearing the decks, spending some time meditating, keeping the chattering mind quiet, is to allow intuition to call, instincts, deeper callings and direction.

'When we give off nothing but busy signals, calls simply don't get through. There's no room for them. Make some room. Get off the line once in a while.'

Callings: Finding and Following an Authentic Life,
GREGG LEVOY

SWITCH TO AWARENESS

The more we become aware the more in focus things become. We feel the benefits of bringing this awareness to every aspect of our lives: while driving, listening to what children or our partner are saying to us; being attentive in a meeting rather than letting the random brain malfunction into rushing ahead through thinking what to say next; listening to music; focusing on what you're reading; and so on. In other words, living life fully without performing so many tasks on autopilot.

This isn't a technique or something that you have to wait years to perfect; it can be done in an instant. You set your mind to it and decide to *be* aware. The challenge that we take up is *staying* in that attention span. Of course we 'forget', as that muscle slackens, but the more we recognise that we've come out of aware-ness, the more we get back into it. It becomes a habit and a sort of enchanting game with oneself. When we see and feel the benefits of it and how life is somehow more real when we know we are living in the instant, the past falls away from us and the future ceases to be something to worry about constantly.

'The more you are focused on time – the past and future – the more you miss the Now, the most precious thing there is.'

The Power of Now:
A Guide to Spiritual Enlightenment,
ECKHART TOLLE

USING OUR THINKING

Unconscious thinking is when we get a blur of random thoughts; conscious thinking is taking a thought and staying with it, with awareness. It might be an idea that we want to sharpen, a piece of creative work that needs fresh inspiration, a mathematical or financial problem that needs solving, or a way to actively brainstorm with ourselves about a particular solution we are seeking.

This idea of selecting a thought to think about is very flexible; we can select one appropriate to the time slot, for some brief conscious *thinking time* in the random 'waiting' slots that arise throughout the day: mindatation. Furthermore, it imbues waiting with positive energy, so instead of becoming stressed at the time lost by a delayed train, queuing or having to wait for a meeting to start, or waiting for a visitor, we can actually be relaxed and enjoy concentrating on a particular thought that needs attention. Siddhartha, in Herman Hesse's novel of the same name, when asked what he was good at, said he was good at waiting. And perhaps we can see why.

'"Have you also learned that secret from the river; that there is no such thing as time?"...

"That the river is everywhere at the same time, at the source and at the mouth, at the waterfall, at the ferry, at the current, in the ocean and in the mountains, everywhere and that the present only exists for it, not the shadow of the past nor the shadow of the future?"

"That is it," said Siddhartha.'

Siddhartha,
HERMANN HESSE

Another way of trying to describe time awareness (although it is different for different people) is taking the analogy of opening up the windows of our mind to let in the light. And if we use the eyes and ears of our mind to be super-tuned into what's going on around us, we will find unexpected joy and clarity.

Stop for a moment and do that, to experience the clarity.

Stop and see what is around you, what sounds you hear, what you are literally aware of.

BUDDHA:

> When you eat, eat.
> When you walk, walk.
> When you sleep, sleep.

This is a good reminder of the simplicity of awareness and of focusing on one thing at a time.

Using our breathing

An easily accessible, and constantly available, way of practising the art of awareness is using the breath. Not using complicated breathing exercises, but just this: take a decent-sized breath all the way in and all the way out. Then let the breathing settle down. All the while, just focus on the breath. Nothing else. This is awareness.

When it finds its own natural rhythm, just continue to follow each breath: in, then out, and so on.

You cannot be more present than that. After all, you cannot breathe in the past and you cannot experience breathing in the future – you can only breathe in the present time.

While your breathing is strengthening your awareness muscle, it is relaxing you. It is a wonderful way to get off to sleep and can be used in any small break for a few minutes here and there throughout your day to de-stress, to return to the calm pool.

FIND A REMINDER

Mantras are good ways of reminding ourselves throughout the day to keep coming back to the moment of time that we're in. They don't need to be allied to meditation or spirituality of any kind, they can be 'secular' mantras. They could be a name or a particular word you like the sound of, or a word that evokes a good feeling. After a while the reflex of mentally saying the word pops into your head at unexpected moments, which is the reminder we need to return our thinking to the present, to become untangled in thoughts that have become jumbled and to take a moment to breathe and drop our shoulders in a moment of relaxation. 'Catching our breath ...'

And at that point, significantly and relishing in the importance of doing so, we can re-evaluate our time expenditure. How do we want to spend this moment ... and this one, and the now-moments to come?

Those who keep flexible remain the freest: not to be locked into more time schedules than we have to. This gives us the greater amount of choice of how to spend our time – when the time comes.

Whatever, wherever and however life has taken us to get up to the present moment . . .

this is where we are . . .
now

And this, dear reader, is the most important part of the book. In fact it's the most important part of your life, since, as you're reading these words, it is precisely, and the *only*, place in space and time in which you exist.

'Ah, now! That odd time, the oddest time of all times, the time it always is… by the time we've reached the "w" of "now" the "n" is ancient history.'

Constructions,
MICHAEL FRAYN

NOW-TIME

We cannot count on forward time to be a certainty, but we can count on the now moment, the present moment as a certainty, so that's the one to be in. Another way of looking at this is being aware of being surrounded by the present moment. This is not just the millisecond-now but the general-now: the few moments or minutes that make up what we perceive to be the now moment. The hour that we're in, the day that we're in . . . the present part of our lives that we're living. Soon we come to see that time is an endless succession of 'nows': the eternal present.

Whereas it's important to plan, we tend to become weighed down by plans, then tied in knots as to the possible outcomes and permutations that become yet more mired in the fantasy of expectation. And the more we go down that route, the more we set ourselves up for possible disappointment.

Try not to be weighed down by planning, but incorporate it into our now moment as an active, conscious part of our present.

And, importantly, are you, now, where you wanted your planning to bring you?

HOW LONG IS NOW?

Most people have experienced sitting in the window seat of a train and watching the landscape race past them.

There is, in that activity, the sense of truly capturing the future, the present and the past. One moment the view ahead of us is somehow in the future, then it is in front of us, representing the fleeting present, before it disappears behind us and into the past. And we can turn our heads and actually *see* that past!

Recent studies by neuroscientists suggest that 'now' lasts a couple of seconds: about the same time as the captured view from the train window.

BEING AWARE OF THE
DECISIONS WE MAKE

Can we be *cash-rich* and *time-rich* at the same time? If not, there is a big decision to make. Which takes priority?

To be *cash-rich* and *time-poor*?

Or,

To be *time-rich* and *cash-poor*?

Don't dwell on these questions, but if you had to answer the question quickly, which would you choose? That's your inner voice guiding you. We can instantly see where our priorities are by looking at the simple answer to a simple question. This could be the basis for organising our lives in such a way as to make us happy – or at least happier.

You might have read this story before, based on the original by Heinrich Böll, but it is worth re-reading it in light of being cash-rich or time-rich.

One day a fisherman was lying on a beautiful beach, with his fishing pole propped up in the sand and his solitary line cast out into the sparkling blue surf. He was enjoying the warmth of the afternoon Sun and the prospect of catching a fish.

About that time, a businessman came walking down the beach trying to relieve some of the stress of his work day. He noticed the fisherman sitting on the beach and decided to find out why this fisherman was fishing instead of working harder to make a living for himself and his family. 'You aren't going to catch many fish that way,' said the businessman. 'You should be working rather than lying on the beach!'

The fisherman looked up at the businessman, smiled and replied, 'And what will my reward be?'

'Well, you can get bigger nets and catch more fish!' was the businessman's answer.

'And then what will my reward be?' asked the fisherman, still smiling.

The businessman replied, 'You will make money

and you'll be able to buy a boat, which will then result in larger catches of fish!'

'And then what will my reward be?' asked the fisherman again.

The businessman was beginning to get a little irritated with the fisherman's questions. 'You can buy a bigger boat, and hire some people to work for you!' he said.

'And then what will my reward be?' repeated the fisherman.

The businessman was getting angry. 'Don't you understand? You can build up a fleet of fishing boats, sail all over the world, and let all your employees catch fish for you!'

Once again the fisherman asked, 'And then what will my reward be?'

The businessman was red with rage and shouted at the fisherman, 'Don't you understand that you can become so rich that you will never have to work for your living again! You can spend all the rest of your days sitting on this beach, looking at the sunset. You won't have a care in the world!'

The fisherman, still smiling, looked up and said, 'And what do you think I'm doing right now?'

'Nothing keeps. There is one law in the universe: NOW.'

The Open Door,
ALFRED SUTRO

FIND THE QUEST WITHIN YOU

Take time to find your quest. It's a way of getting to know yourself better to let free the true you. I'm not talking about riding into the night sky on a white horse to discover unknown distant planets (necessarily!) but realistic, positive quests that are within one's physical and terrestrial capabilities. This could be anything from learning the art of archery, becoming a magician in your spare time, taking up homeopathy, learning the language of the country you like best, finally taking that longed-for journey, or deciding to change your whole life and work structure.

Compare your quest to your present life. How many similarities are there? Are there any? Is it time to bring some of those quest aspects into our lives so that we can incrementally enjoy them, until we realise that there is nothing to stop us embarking on our quests alone or with loved ones?

There are plenty of instances where families have taken a month, a year, a lifetime, perhaps following a quest, and reconnecting them to the fundamental importance of life and its natural rhythms.

'You must live in the present, launch yourself on every wave, find your eternity in each moment.'

HENRY DAVID THOREAU

If taking off, or going back to nature in the following of Henry Thoreau and others is a step too far, there are many other ways of changing pace, slowing down, being aware and enjoying the continuous moment, which is time itself.

Work out what it is that you want or need. Then set about doing it or finding it.

SOLUTIONS

Even partial solutions and explorations are more positive than waiting, procrastinating and indecision. If circumstances don't appear to be perfect (they never are, there's always uncertainty in every undertaking) it is better to participate in the current of life if the inclination is there than wait for preconceived plans to take shape.

Success comes from building on small things.

'Until one is committed, there is hesitancy, the chance to draw back, always ineffectiveness. Concerning all acts of initiative and creation, there is one elementary truth the ignorance of which kills countless ideas and splendid plans: that the moment one definitely commits oneself, then providence moves too.

All sorts of things occur to help one that would never otherwise have occurred. A whole stream of events issues from the decision, raising in one's favour all manner of unforeseen incidents, meetings and material assistance which no man could have dreamed would have come his way.

Whatever you can do or dream you can, begin it. Boldness has genius, power and magic in it. Begin it now.'

JOHANN WOLFGANG VON GOETHE

BRUTUS:

> There is a tide in the affairs of men.
> Which, taken at the flood, leads on
>   to fortune;
> Omitted, all the voyage of their life
> Is bound in shallows and in miseries.
> On such a full sea are we now afloat,
> And we must take the current when
>   it serves,
> Or lose our ventures.

Julius Caesar, Act 4, Scene 3: 218–24,

WILLIAM SHAKESPEARE

Brutus and Cassius are discussing the final phase of their civil war with the forces of Octavian and Marcus Antonius. Cassius has been urging that they group their forces at Sardis and take advantage of the secure location to catch their breath. Brutus, however, advocates heading off the enemy at Philippi before Octavian can recruit more men.

Brutus's main point is that, since 'the enemy increaseth every day' and 'We, at the height, are ready to decline' (lines 216–17), he and Cassius must act now while the ratio of forces is most advantageous. 'There is a tide in the affairs of men,' he insists; that is, power is a force that ebbs and flows in time, and one must 'go with the flow'. Waiting around only allows your power to pass its crest and begin to ebb. If the opportunity is 'omitted' (missed), you'll find yourself stranded in miserable shallows.

'There are really four dimensions, three
which we call the three planes of Space,
and a fourth, Time.'

The Time Machine,
H.G. WELLS

TIME TRAVEL

Paul Davies, professor of physics at Arizona University, says that a hundred years ago the idea of space travel was the stuff of science fiction, but now space travel is commonplace; however, time travel seems to us still the stuff of science fiction, but might it be that in a hundred years, or even less, time travel will be as commonplace – and as possible – as space travel has now become?

The laws of nature do not prohibit time travel, but to build a time machine we still need to understand more about those laws. Scientists continue to work on discoveries to date, looking at ways to build wormholes, how to manipulate entangled photons and to stretch time in different directions – enough to enable an engineer of the not-too-distant future to build a machine that would allow us to travel back and forward in time at the touch of a button.

ADAPTED FROM THE PROFILE OF
THE BBC *HORIZON* PROGRAMME,
'HOW TO BUILD A TIME MACHINE'

NOT JUST SCIENCE FICTION

Most of us have experienced some form of 'alternative time' experience, induced or otherwise. There are many apparent, different dimensions of time: when we lose track of time, when we are at that moment when we fall asleep between two worlds, when we dream, when we make love, when we're absorbed in creating a piece of art, playing with children. Athletes, dancers, musicians, mountain climbers – the list is long and personal to each of us in the ways in which we can experience an absolute oneness with the present moment.

SETTLING TO SLEEP

Sleep is another portal through which we can cross over to non-global time – time travel of a different kind. It is worthwhile preparing for this nightly adventure. Once you've eventually got your pillow right and are lying in a comfortable position, settle into spending a few moments skimming through the day before you switch off your brain for the night. Register the key events or people, ideas or developments the day has provided to make sure that you haven't missed anything you'd like to take forward with you or bring with you to the following day. 'Skim' is the key word here – don't go off on tangents of what-ifs and whys, just simply register it objectively. If it's been a hectic day and you find it difficult to switch off the thinking brain, lie flat and do a total body check. Relax each part of your body bit by bit, breath by breath.

SLEEP TIME

Sleep, and what happens in our brains and subconscious, remains a fascinating, yet elusive, enigma despite the fact that we have been climbing into bed every night of our lives to experience it.

We spend (roughly) a third of our lives asleep! If we live to be 90, that's *30* years time-wise spent asleep. Or, in a year, that's four months asleep! That's a lot of subconscious material, potentially precious nuggets of advice and information, and a lot of dreaming. And our dreams are so random and unpredictable yet full of influence over the day to come.

What goes on in that sleep time? What goes on in those (eventual and approximate) 30 years of our lives? Can we utilise this precious time more productively? Can we harness our conscious minds somehow to access the subconscious dream faculty? Can we influence how we dream and, in doing so, ensure a more relaxed day ahead (and therefore better use of the day's time)? Do we go to sleep, as modern science suggests, primarily seeking respite and restoration from the challenges of waking life?

Many of us tend to skip over sleep as something that gets done in the night hours because we've been taught to equate it with a vague time in which our bodies can rest and heal. Although that is a valid reason for sleep, we also have the choice of remaining open to the idea of sleep as a nightly return to another time dominion, by bringing more mindfulness to bed.

HAMLET:

To be, or not to be: that is the question:
Whether 'tis nobler in the mind to suffer
The slings and arrows of outrageous
      fortune,
Or to take Arms against a Sea of troubles,
And by opposing end them? To die: to sleep;
No more; and by a sleep, to say we end
The heart-ache, and the thousand
      natural shocks
That Flesh is heir to? 'Tis a consummation
Devoutly to be wish'd. To die, to sleep;
To sleep: perchance to Dream: ay,
      there's the rub;
For in that sleep of death what
      dreams may come
When we have shuffled off this mortal coil,
Must give us pause.

Hamlet, Act 3, Scene 1,
WILLIAM SHAKESPEARE

LUCID DREAMING

There are various practices that we can consider. One of them is to develop lucid dreaming. The definition of lucid dreaming is actually quite simple: it is being lucid, or aware, during a dream; however, the deeper understanding of this and how to achieve it requires some individual research. There are many books and websites to explore on the subject. Basic preparation for sleep, though, remains essential: not watching violent films or news clips before bed, and not dealing with emails, work issues or anything negative that will become the last thing you think about before sleep.

Certain foods are best avoided – in fact, any heavy eating and drinking late in the evening. Even though we know this to be true and good advice, we all too often and too easily overlook it. But we also know from experience that we will regret it the following day, because it leads to disturbed sleep or dreams, or both.

If you want to influence your dreams in a particular direction, train yourself to become fully immersed in a landscape of your choosing that will promote a calm and restful sense of being.

For more insightful access to our dreams and sleep, practising yoga or other meditative practices, including mindfulness, during the day will contribute greatly towards sound sleep – and clearer tomorrows.

'The dream is the liberation of the spirit from the pressure of external nature, a detachment of the soul from the fetters of matter.'

The Interpretation of Dreams,
SIGMUND FREUD

MINDFULNESS MEDITATIONS

Practising awareness, bringing ourselves back to 'being aware' at any moment during the day, will lead to a more continuous, seamless awareness, including, carrying ourselves back and forth into our subconscious more effectively and readily. Implementing a 20-minute mindfulness meditation into your daily routine not only empowers your day time but it also increases your chances of experiencing lucid dreams.

The more we practise random mindfulness or meditation, the more accustomed and the more easily we can slip into awareness on all its levels, such as focusing on our work, being more patient and compassionate towards others, and maximising our sleep potential.

In the morning, as you stretch out and unfurl from the night, be aware of coming back out of subconscious time to conscious thinking. Look at the new now, to having this new roster of 24 hours to plan. Use this early morning time to make a structure on which to hang the day. Doing this means that you can come back to the structure if you need stabilising, or a reminder of your goals or intentions. It frees you to being able to stay in awareness, and living consciously.

Try to emerge more slowly into the day instead of leaving the alarm set for the last minute. This allows you to stride more purposefully into the day, more thoughtfully, and avoids being frazzled before 10am.

When you're on holiday, or lucky enough to have a few days free, try sleeping with natural night – going to bed when it gets dark and getting up at first light to enjoy a return to natural time flow.

There are Tibetan yoga meditations of dream and sleep, which are not quick fixes but a particular yoga practice intended to access the subconscious and the time that we are asleep. Perhaps one of the simplest poses to help attain consciousness in our dreams is **Visualising the Dream**.

Firstly, adjust your position so that your spine is straight and your head and neck in alignment. Adjust your breathing so that it is calm and regular.

Begin this meditation by taking a deep breath from the base of your lungs and then draw your breath up and around as though in a semi-circle, in a convex movement until you get to the top. Hold it for a moment and then gently expel your breath as though coming down on the other side of the circle in a concave movement until you get to the end of the breath. Hold it again until it naturally wants to repeat the movement: in, up, hold, out, down, hold.

After a while your breath follows this natural rhythm. Then you can watch this breath, be aware of it, follow it.

Now that you are calm and focused, you are ready to visualise your dream. Bring your dream into the awareness you are experiencing with your breath. Whatever it is – to be on the beach of your dreams, to be with the person you love, to be travelling into space or exploring the depths of the ocean – whatever your dream is, now is the time to hold it and not let it go. Hold it and start exploring it with each movement of the breath. When you find your mind drifting to other areas, bring your mind back to the awareness of the breath and your dream will come too.

By simply paying attention to each of these movements, eventually you will drift off to sleep and your dream will take you with it.

'Through practice we can cultivate greater awareness during every moment of life. If we do, freedom and flexibility continually increase and we are less governed by habitual preoccupations and distractions. We develop a stable and vivid presence that allows us to more skilfully choose positive responses to whatever arises, responses that best benefit others and our own spiritual journey. Eventually we develop a continuity of awareness that allows us to maintain full awareness during dream as well as in waking life.'

TENZIN WANGYAL RINPOCHE

MEDITATION IN BED

Make time before sleep.

You have time in the night if you wake.

Make a little time after sleep.

Practising daily meditation or mindfulness for a few minutes brings us back to the present moment. It keeps us aware, open to possibilities, alert to good fortune and prepared in times of need, and it is vital for our well-being.

'Chance is always powerful. Let your hook be always cast; in the pool where you least expect it, there will be a fish.'

Heroides,
OVID

ART IN TIME

We are surrounded by visual art – in galleries and museums but also in the posters and ads that promote the exhibitions. We see art in offices, hospitals, hotels and our own homes. But how much of it do we digest? We are bombarded with images in advertising, packaging, on-screen news and film, and across social media. We rarely have time to stop and distinguish between finer art and applied arts or between authentic images and those that are airbrushed.

Good art has a way of absorbing us, taking us into it, taking us out of temporality – a form of meditation perhaps. If we are fortunate enough to be near a public museum or art gallery, we can take time out of a busy day to go inside and find a work of art that appeals to us. Instead of hurrying from one piece to another, stop and enjoy one piece, become absorbed in it, give it time. Spend perhaps five or ten minutes focusing on it and noticing the feelings it brings out in you.

We can do the same at home, spending time engaging with one piece that you walk past daily but never stop to really notice after a while. There are also many wonderful websites for viewing paintings and sculpture on your laptop; for example, the National Gallery, MOMA, the Guggenheim, and any number of other small or large galleries that display art on their websites.

AN ART EXERCISE TO
SHARPEN THE SENSES

Take one of your pictures or a pot, a bowl of shells, a piece of driftwood you have collected or a piece of nature's sculpture, and take it to where you like to sit and meditate. Set your timer (actual or imagined) for 15 minutes and just sit still and absorb the piece of art, the story it tells you, the colours, the shades, the atmosphere. If you start to think 'outside' the item, bring yourself gently back 'inside' it and continue with your meditation.

Still lifes in art offer a way of slowing down the mind and the attention – a meditation in awareness.

Mandalas are ancient forms of art on which to meditate, almost certainly created as far back as the fourth century by Buddhist monks. The symmetrical, concentric circles, shapes and patterns of the art are designed to ease the overloaded mind and release its deep-rooted creative and expressive inclination – a form of meditation in which time-related pressures are precluded.

'It is looking at things for a long time that ripens you and gives you a deeper meaning.'

VINCENT VAN GOGH

THE CHANGE OF SEASONS

In Japan there is a conscious observation of the time and change of each season. In many homes, the pieces of art are moved around in order for the inhabitants to be aware of the changing seasons: the leaves as they turn colour outside or any other aspect of nature changing around them. A specific place in the home might be designated to have a different artwork at each new season. It's a beautiful and appropriate way of observing time.

'We have so much time and so little to do.
Strike that, reverse it.'

Charlie and the Great Glass Elevator,
ROALD DAHL

MAÑANA

Procrastination is one of the ways we deal with time, by projecting something into future time and avoiding dealing with it in the present.

It would be a significantly focused and dedicated person who never procrastinated. It is, essentially, deviating from the task in hand to do something more pleasurable (or less tedious).

But we are not automatons (yet) and need to recognise good procrastination from bad; for example, if you are struggling to finish a paper with only a day left in which to do it, it is sometimes the right thing to do to go and walk around the block, go for a jog, make that cup of coffee or ginger zinger in order to come back to the work refreshed.

The key is making an honest choice. To stop what you're doing out of laziness, fidgetiness or boredom might be the wrong choice and will require a mental adjustment to click yourself back on track, but if there is a genuine block, a build-up of too many distractions beyond your control or your body telling you that you legitimately need to take five, the break will be a good use of time: ten minutes out, in order to achieve another couple of focused hours instead of winding down to non-productivity. It's a question of making informed choices. Cause and effect. And it all comes back to awareness.

Choose one thing over which you procrastinate most, such as tidying the kitchen, doing monthly accounts, making difficult phone calls. Whatever it is, identify it and try to 'overcome' it. A great source of satisfaction will follow (as well as getting those things done).

A loose amble, on the other hand, is an alternative structure, or non-structure, for the day, because perhaps we're on holiday, or because I want to freewheel, or I'm having a day off and simply want to see where the day takes me. Being a conscious ambler is different from being an unconscious procrastinator!

TIME-MANAGEMENT TECHNIQUES

The following time-management exercises might not appeal to you for being overly commanding, but there might be something to pluck from these somewhat dry prescriptions. I personally benefited from the Pomodora technique while working on parts of this book.

POSEC

An acronym for Prioritise by Organising, Streamlining, Economising and Contributing, the POSEC method dictates a template that emphasises an average individual's immediate sense of emotional and monetary security. It suggests that by attending to one's personal responsibilities first, an individual is better positioned to shoulder collective responsibilities:

Prioritise your time and define your life by goals.

Organise things you have to accomplish regularly to be successful (family and finances).

Streamline things you might not like to do, but must do (work and chores).

Economise things you should do, or might even like to do, but which aren't pressingly urgent (pastimes and socialising).

Contribute by paying attention to the few remaining things that make a difference (social obligations) – the implementation of goals.

POMODORO TECHNIQUE

The Pomodoro Technique is a time-management method developed by Francesco Cirillo in the late 1980s. The exercise uses a timer to break down work into intervals, traditionally 25 minutes in length, separated by short breaks. These intervals are named pomodoros, the plural in English of the Italian word *pomodoro* (tomato) after the tomato-shaped kitchen timer that Cirillo used when he was a university student.

There are five steps in the technique:

1. Decide on the task to be done, and the length of time you want your pomodoros to be.
2. Set the pomodoro (or any timer – although there is something compelling about the physicality of a wind-up kitchen timer over a phone app. And you can buy, quite cheaply, the original red tomato-shaped timer. The physical act of winding the timer confirms the user's determination to

start the task; the ticking externalises the desire to complete the task; the ringing announces a break.

3. Work on the task until the timer rings. If a distraction pops into your head, write it down, but immediately get back on task.
4. After the timer rings, put a check mark on a piece of paper.
5. After four pomodoros (100 minutes) take a longer break (15–30 minutes), reset your check mark, count to zero, then start again.

For the purposes of the technique, a pomodoro is the interval of time spent working. After task completion, any time remaining in the pomodoro is devoted to recapping what has been done or learned in that time. Regular breaks are taken, aiding assimilation. A short (3–5 minutes) rest separates consecutive pomodoros. Four pomodoros form a set. A longer (15–30 minute) rest is taken between sets.

ABC ANALYSIS

A technique that has been used in business management for a long time is the categorisation of large data into groups. These groups are often marked A, B and C – hence the name. Activities are ranked by these general criteria:

A Tasks that are perceived as being urgent and important.
B Tasks that are important but not urgent.
C Tasks that are unimportant (whether urgent or not).

Each group is then rank-ordered by priority. To further refine the prioritisation, some individuals choose to then force-rank all the 'B' items as either 'A' or 'C'. ABC analysis can incorporate more than three groups.

ABC analysis is frequently combined with Pareto analysis.

PARETO ANALYSIS

This principle is used to sort tasks into two parts. This is the idea that 80 per cent of tasks can be completed in 20 per cent of the disposable time. The remaining 20 per cent of tasks will take up 80 per cent of the time. According to this form of Pareto analysis it is recommended that tasks that fall into the first category be assigned a higher priority.

TIPS FOR A MORE PRODUCTIVE DAY

Practise some of the following techniques to become the master of your own time:

1. Record all your thoughts, conversations and activities for a week. You'll see how much time is spent on actually producing results and how much time is wasted on unproductive thoughts, conversations and actions.
2. Schedule appointments with yourself and create time blocks for high-priority thoughts, conversations and actions. Some people even schedule for 'worry' times where a specific issue is thought over so that worry doesn't spill over into general thinking. Have the discipline to keep these appointments.
3. Schedule time for interruptions. Plan time to be pulled away from what you're doing.
4. Take the first 10 to 30 minutes of every day to plan your day. Don't start your day until you complete your time plan.

5. Take a few minutes before every important call and task to decide what result you want to attain. This will help you to focus and to know what success looks like before you start. Take five minutes after each call and activity to determine whether your desired result was achieved. If not, what was missing? How do you put what's missing in your next activity?

6. Put up a 'Do not disturb' sign (on your door or on your phone) when you absolutely have to get work done.

7. Practise not answering the phone just because it's ringing and emails just because they show up.

8. Disconnect instant messaging. Don't instantly give people your attention unless it's absolutely crucial in your business to offer an immediate human response.

9. Block out other distractions such as social media unless you use these tools to generate business.

10. It's impossible to get everything done. The odds are good that 20 per cent of your thoughts, conversations and activities produce 80 per cent of your results.

LIGHTEN THE SOCIAL LOAD

Are you often stressed by the amount of commitments and activities you have agreed to and then must follow through?

When put on the spot and asked to do something we know immediately we don't want to do, many of us find it hard to say a straight no. Very few people say, 'No thanks, I don't want to come/go/do it.' We can often feel we have to give an excuse, and if we don't have one on the tip of our tongue then we have accepted by implication.

We can get into such busy habits of spending our weekends in a particular way – brunch here, shopping, window-shopping, house-cleaning, DIY, seeing people (see above!) – that sometimes it's important to call 'time' and cut loose from mere habit and to spend time doing very little, totally relaxing, doing what we (selfishly) want to do – or at least spending time exploring all the other options available for a fulfilling weekend.

Most of us are invited to join this, pledge for that, run for the other, either directly by friends, family and colleagues or through websites that we have joined either consciously or through our use of online shopping or online participation. We are bombarded by emails that don't fall into our email trash but pop up as a result of our signing up for (unwanted) newsletters, and they seem to refuse to go away. Sites we have shopped in are constantly coming back to us like traders on market stalls, calling out their wares and begging us to shop with them again . . . and again.

We might procrastinate in clearing our computer cookies, our emails, or other types of communication but the importance of this is clear in order not to be swamped by these time-poor drainers.

Tristan Harris, a former Google designer and founder of the Time Well Spent movement, has radical ideas to harness our screen time, putting only basic tools such as a calendar and camera on your phone's home screen. If you want to access YouTube, for example, you can easily access it via Google/your Internet server, instead of having the app icon subliminally tempting you.

Your time is your own.
What a wonderful and freeing
thought that is.
Enjoy it.
Let go ... swim with it, flow with it ...

Let every man be master of his time.

Macbeth, Act 3, Scene I,
WILLIAM SHAKESPEARE

Of what percentage of the day, the week or your life, can you say, '*My time is my own*'?

It might be advantageous to think about this and see if you can raise the percentage in order to have more time that you can call your own.

Guard against the tide of computer technology and biometric sensors accessing our minds to a point where computers might come to understand us better than we understand ourselves. Our free will and with it how we choose to spend our time – our days, our lives – is being eroded with sci-fi reality. Only by being aware of this can we even begin to be sure that we can stay in control of our own direction instead of allowing the rise of tech companies to collect our data and gain ever-increasing insights into our minds.

So it follows that managing our attention, and becoming aware of who the powers are that orchestrate these technological invasions, has to lie with us – while we still can.

WATCHING TIME GROW

You can actually see bamboo grow. If you spent the day watching it you would *actually see time grow.* I asked landscape and forest gardener extraordinaire Martin Crawford, who first introduced me to this fact, whether he had tried it. The irony was that Martin said he didn't have the time to stop and watch it (time) grow!

Hi Tiddy,

Bamboo shoots in the UK summer grow about 1cm/hour in hot weather – it is possible to see them growing though surprisingly difficult to stay concentrated enough to achieve that! It is more noticeable to hear them growing, as the shoot tips expand and the leafy sheaths crackle and open.

Best regards,
Martin Crawford, Agroforestry Research Trust

What a great meditation practice that would be!

SOME IDEAS WHEN YOU ARE TIME-SHORT

Stuck in traffic?

1. Focus on your breathing and posture.
2. Lengthen up through the back of the neck.
3. Soften the jaw and throat.
4. Breathe in for five and out for five.

Waiting in a queue? Waiting for the lift? Waiting on the platform for your train?

1. Start with your feet planted firmly on the ground and consciously work your way up through your body, relaxing each area.
2. Sway almost imperceptibly gently backwards and forwards until you find a happy spot for your weight through your feet.
3. Relax your knees.
4. Tilt your pelvis marginally up and down until you find a happy place.

5. Breathe into the stomach, release any tension in the spine, shoulders and neck as you exhale.
6. Feel your arms heavy by your side.

(These movements do not need to be exaggerated. In fact, sometimes less conspicuous movements lead to a slower and more relaxed flow.)

HUMAN TIME VS SPIRIT/SOUL/ UNIVERSAL TIME

We rush around in 'temporal' time, global time, but meditation gives us a chance to access timelessness – non-global time, other time, universe time, eternal time – a time in which our spirit/soul can operate uncluttered by the din of daily noise.

We can learn to slip into that no-man's time that hangs between the time on the kitchen clock and the time by the size of the Moon. That time is unaccounted for, hidden, secret, when we can lie in the hammocks of our minds.

Practising mindfulness is something we can more easily access during the 'global' times in a day, as it is a trigger to bring us back to our breathing and our awareness – the link back to the spirit to keep the two, body and spirit, as harmonious as possible. Building the habit of meditation for a dedicated few minutes, 10, 15, 20 or more, on a regular basis will guide you naturally to that other time-space where your deeper, inner voice has a chance to be heard.

'Time is dead as long as it is being clicked off by little wheels; only when the clock stops does time come to life'

The Sound and the Fury,
WILLIAM FAULKNER

TIMING

There is another relative in the family of *time*, and that is *timing*.

I am fascinated by watching powerful surfers far out in the water poised for the big waves breaking in from the Atlantic. Their patience is praiseworthy, their focus, their attention – their awareness. They might wait for ages and ages, and then suddenly they stand up on their boards and swoop in on the crest of a giant wave. If they catch it, if their timing is absolutely at one with that breaking wave, the ride is sublime. Often, of course, the timing is off by a millionth of a second and they fall into the white surf and then have to plough their way out again . . . and again and again.

'You can't stop the waves, but you can learn to surf.'

JON KABAT-ZINN

The surfers remind me of the herons or the kingfisher I used to watch on an estuary: they would wait so long and so patiently until the timing was right, when they swooped and snatched the fish.

'Time is a kind of river, an irresistible flood sweeping up men and events and carrying them headlong, one after the other, to the great sea of being.'

Meditations,
MARCUS AURELIUS

Timing is relevant to so many aspects of our doing and our being in life. We talk about the 'timing of things' and 'when the time is right' and somehow, miraculously even, the timing is more often right than not, especially when we become more and more tuned in to that timing. When we succeed, it is more than likely because we have caught the timing at its nexus. Then again, if we don't think that things have gone in our favour, how often do we rant against results only to realise later on that the timing *was* right and the outcome was favourable, but we just didn't realise it or see it at the time? This after-knowledge increases our confidence in continuing with that all-important flow and trusting the process.

LIFE ITSELF IS LIKE A DANCE

Life is a dance, and so the time and timing is of vital importance to keep balanced, to keep in rhythm, to keep in time. Maybe that's why when we feel good we feel in step, we feel in time. And let's be playful. Dance isn't all about one speed, there are slow parts and fast parts and twirly bits. There is something instinctive that happens when we dance, putting us in touch with a natural beat, following an unprescribed rhythm.

As Samuel Beckett has Estragon say in *Waiting for Godot*, 'dance first and think afterwards', being the natural order of things. And, after all, we all know that feeling of liberation to dance unfettered, but the moment we think too much our feet get in a tangle and we lose the natural rhythm. Let life be a dance, too.

MINDFULNESS AND MEDITATION

If meditation takes us into that other timelessness, mindfulness is the connector that allows us to keep one foot in temporal-human time and one foot in eternal time. Through mindfulness we become practised at returning, often, to the breath, which triggers our muscle of awareness and *connects* our body and spirit-essence.

When we stop and are completely still, we become unaware of time; time has no relevance for us.

It's a good reason to meditate, and for which we must make, or find, a space that is still and quiet.

What are days for?
Days are where we live.
They come, they wake us
Time and time over.
They are to be happy in:
Where can we live but days?

Ah, solving that question
Brings the priest and the doctor
In their long coats
Running over the fields.

'Days',
PHILIP LARKIN

WE HAVE GOT TIME

It's not true to say that we haven't got time. We have an abundance of it on a daily basis – as long as we have life and therefore time itself, paradoxically – but it's more a question of what we choose to *do* with our time. If you say, 'I haven't got time' if someone asks you to join their book club or go to the cinema or have a drink, it really means 'I don't want to, because, in fact, I choose to do something else.' What about duty, you might say? Well, it's still a *choice* isn't it?

'Those who make the worst use of their time are the first to complain of its brevity.'

Les Caractères,
JEAN DE LA BRUYÈRE

TIME AND TAO

Followers along the path of Tao are not looking for longevity as a final requirement. For them, the term 'longevity' means not so much wishing to live forever as focusing on their determination to live the course of their lives to the fullest. Longevity looked at in this light reminds us that it is the quality of the time that we have that is important – the means not the end.

Ageing is a natural process; the passing of relative time is inevitable. We only have to look at nature to observe this: the seed of an apple tree that grows, flowers, gives fruit and eventually withers. Even where time is considered an illusion there is the cycle of life, which demonstrates the passing of the observable passage of 'time'. Becoming more aware of this in nature reminds us, gently, of how and why we need to savour each moment, each decade, each stage of our lives.

We are more acutely aware of this ageing process as we get older, when the life span ahead of us may be on the horizon rather than the distant myth it appears to be in our youth. Time changes us according to our

metabolism, our life experiences, our sense of fulfilment so far and the desire to spend time differently;
the instinctive response to slowing down, perhaps, in
order to savour better the time we have.

'Sometimes when I meet old friends, it reminds me how quickly time passes. And it makes me wonder if we've utilised our time properly or not. Proper utilisation of time is so important. While we have this body, and especially this amazing human brain, I think every minute is something precious. Our day-to-day existence is very much alive with hope, although there is no guarantee of our future. There is no guarantee that tomorrow at this time we will be here. But we are working for that purely on the basis of hope. So, we need to make the best use of our time. I believe that the proper utilisation of time is this: if you can, serve other people, other sentient beings. If not, at least refrain from harming them. I think that is the whole basis of my philosophy.

'So, let us reflect what is truly of value in life, what gives meaning to our lives, and set our priorities on the basis of that. The purpose of our life needs to be

positive. We weren't born with the purpose
of causing trouble, harming others. For
our life to be of value, I think we must
develop basic good human qualities –
warmth, kindness, compassion. Then
our life becomes meaningful and more
peaceful – happier.'

The Art of Happiness,
DALAI LAMA XIV

GROWING OLDER

In an age of increased longevity, more of us can expect to celebrate our hundredth birthday than in the past. Identifying with 'middle age' has rapidly changed from our late thirties to a more realistic forties/fifties age group. The whole idea of a 'midlife crisis', then, might not hit until we're fifty when many people are also looking towards retirement.

With a general rise in good health and medical resources, older people being wealthier and healthier for longer should mean that there will be no crisis to experience. As we grow older today we are generally better equipped, better informed and have access to better health treatment.

Because of the beauty-obsessed culture we live in, however, a crisis of another age-related group kicks in earlier, leading to Botox, surgery, hair and teeth implants – or a loss of confidence. We are persuaded that the way we look has a greater bearing on how we feel about ourselves, so in a way it is a confidence crisis that we are facing. But instead of enduring these 'crises', we can spend valuable time tackling the problem from the inside out (rather than the outside in). Coming to terms with life itself – and the fact of our own mortality – will give us far greater illumination, energy, vitality, benefits and joy that will see us flow from one age group to another.

Behavioural economists, including the Nobel Prize winner, Angus Deaton, posit that 'life satisfaction tends to decline gradually after early adulthood, bottom out in middle age, then gradually rebound after' (quoted from a review in 'Books – Life and Arts', *Weekend FT* 14 July 2018).

If we live to be of a great age, we should consider ourselves to be the lucky ones. How we go about arriving there, and continuing *life satisfaction*, is largely up to us and the choices we make now. That way we will have no regrets.

A time to be born, and a time to die, a time to sow, and a time to reap.

ECCLESIASTES, 3:2

ACCURACY

Every day our lives grow shorter by 24 hours in human clock time. We must make every decision and choice count, in order to keep focused on what we visualise and to accomplish it with the greatest precision. It is vital, therefore, for us to identify our goals and needs, our hopes and ambitions, and to aim for them with the accuracy of an archer's arrow.

There are, essentially, two ways of identifying those hopes and dreams:

1. By putting specific time aside to consciously consider what we want, need or are able to do in life.
2. By putting specific time aside to meditate (or whatever our personal equivalent is of stilling our minds) to let the subconscious search out what those hopes are. Our subconscious 'knows' us better than anyone – even sometimes our conscious selves – so, time spent letting that compass guide us is time well spent.

TIME AND CIRCULAR SPACE

Thinking about the eternal present and then the future, and the endlessness of the past before us, takes us into a way of looking at time that is more *circular* than *linear*. Who among us doesn't believe that the future is not going to happen? I'm pretty sure tomorrow is going to happen. We are hot-wired to believe in it. In any case, future time will continue with or without us. We know it's going to go on (so in that sense the future does exist; it's an axiomatic truth).

If we take this to be ongoing tomorrow and tomorrow and tomorrow, and then look back to the yesterdays beyond our own lives, our parents' lives and the yesterdays of their parents and beyond in endless yesterdays, and if you put those two thoughts together, the endless yesterdays, the eternal present and the endless tomorrows, time is eternal – and possibly even circular. Could that explain why we have glimpses of the past – and the future?

Horace, probably the greatest poet of Roman antiquity, observed:

You must be wise. Pour the wine
and enclose in this brief circle
your long-cherished hope.

THE HUMAN DIMENSION

There is no doubt that a spell of stargazing and reflecting on the vastness of time and space does put our own troubles somewhat into perspective. It helps to put some order into what we consider priorities in our lives and, ultimately, it reminds us how fortunate we are to be in some way a part of it all.

'Looking at these stars suddenly dwarfed my own troubles and all the gravities of terrestrial life. I thought of their unfathomable distance, and the slow inevitable drift of their movements out of the unknown past into the unknown future.'

The Time Machine,
H.G. WELLS

THE HERE AND NOW

Back to today and the here and now.

The here = space, and the now = time.

However much we travel out in space, or back in memories, or forward in imagination, it is the space we're in (here) at this moment (now) that matters most.

We need to keep sieving the past (lightly) so that we don't bring everything with us. We don't have to carry around everything all the time. If we do, it leads us to dwell too much on past issues. For the river to flow freely, stray branches or heavy silt becomes deposited along the bed and the banks, leaving the way forward for the water to flow, clear and clean. Each day we take with us what we need from yesterday, and prepare, just enough, for the way ahead, leaving the present uncluttered where we can live our lives to the fullest.

'Time and tide wait for no man.'

UNKNOWN

In Tao philosophy the centre of anything is an important factor. Where do you instinctively place your hand to indicate the whereabouts of your own centre? Some people place their hands over their heart, the centre of the breastbone, their head or one of the other seven chakras within the body:

The root chakra
The sacral chakra
The solar plexus chakra
The heart chakra
The throat chakra
The third-eye chakra
The crown chakra

Take time to make the connection to your centre. It is where we return to when we need to be re-centred and to regain our balance to gather strength and from which to radiate once again.

PROGRESSION OF LIFE AND CHANGE

The second of July is the central day of the year – in the human-made calendar – with 182 days either side of this day. It is a day to reflect on the centre of things. Being at the centre of anything is to be in a position of strength. In chess, if you dominate the middle board you have the advantage. The eye of a tornado is calm – while turbulence rages around it. So it is when setting out on a project, a journey, a task: if you can identify where the middle of this enterprise is, you will have better control. This puts a new and positive nuance on the notion of middle age.

I am not a Buddhist, yet I embrace the wisdom and insight that comes through many of the teachings. One aspect that is relevant to this centrality is what the Buddha describes as the 'middle way': to be connected to humanity and the world, yet to be able to spend time in solitude, to be inclusive as well as singular, in other words to find the balance in all that we do. When we feel pulled too far in one direction and start to feel out of balance, out of sorts, it is good to return to the centre, *our* centre, recalibrate and continue on our way.

LISTENING OUT FOR THE SLOWER RHYTHMS IN OUR LIVES

The current fast-paced life that we lead takes us away from the natural rhythm of the universe, our own natural circadian rhythm and the natural division of time influenced by the Sun, the Moon, the tides and the seasons: the rhythm of our individual bodies.

Our breathing and heartbeat seek to keep time with the deepest beat of the Earth. We are at our happiest, our most relaxed when we are in harmony – in tune, and in time, with nature. How to discover our own individual optimum pace in life, and how to adapt our lives to that pace, is a matter of taking time, a matter of finding that rhythm, that beat, that awareness by means of a voyage of inner discovery.

*'Time expands, then contracts, all in tune
with the stirrings of the heart.'*

Kafka on the Shore,
HARUKI MURAKAMI

We need slow food, slow living in order to maximise and stretch the moment. There is a tempo and timing in music, in drama, art and literature that we respond to, indicating our likes and dislikes according to our own heartbeat.

It is good to make a list of the slower things in life that we like so that we can be sure to create more time for them. Feasting, fasting, loafing, loving, working, dancing, yoga, swimming, nurturing – it is good, too, to be aware of all the different ways we spend our time in order to find, and keep, a balance in our tempo of life.

'Much better to do fewer things and have time to make the most of them.'

In Praise of Slowness:
Challenging the Cult of Speed,
CARL HONORÉ

How many visual or audio time notifications do we see or hear each day? We cannot go anywhere without being time-hounded and harried, made time-dependent, time-urgent. There is a need to experience time off: taking the watch off, experimenting with non-dependence on what (human-made) time is; taking time out free from imposed time, giving the body, mind and spirit a chance to regain their natural circadian rhythm. How long would it take for the body to find its own body clock again away from temporal conditioning? And where would we need to go to be unaware of clocks – including those on screens, in towns and in shops?

THE ART OF SLOWING DOWN

We live in a culture where rushing around is commonplace, where everyone says to everyone else at some point, and often on a daily basis, 'There isn't enough time to do that or go there', 'The week just flew by without my realising it.' What we don't want is to reach the latter part of our lives and say, 'My *life* just flew by without my realising it.' It's time to slow down and realise this, *really* realise it. It's not a question of putting off that realisation until later on 'when I'll have more time'. The way to create more time is by slowing down and becoming aware of time and aware of not letting it rush away. *The danger is that we always think we will have time.*

Time is the common currency connecting all our lives, like an invisible string that pulls ever tighter, squeezing us and all that we have to do into an ever more stressful grip. If that is what it feels like, it is time to loosen that grip – like loosening the notch on your belt so that you can breathe more easily and live more comfortably.

Slow down. Stop for a while. Look around. Let your

shoulders drop and let your solar plexus consciously relax. Listen to your heartbeat, which is the real body clock ticking away. Breathe as though you are no longer constricted in any way.

Aim for *prosperity in time* over prosperity in money. By making this seemingly simple choice our lives will gradually fall into step with our own natural beat; it will shape our lives in a pattern that we at once recognise and once longed for.

And let's not forget the strength of silence: not to be rushed into answers or reactions but allowing oneself to '*be*', in our own time.

BODY AND SOUL, BUDDHISM

I am drawn to looking for the axis between metaphysics and logic, body and soul, body and mind, between Buddhism and science, between science and spirituality, between theoretical physics and seeking to understand consciousness and something much greater than ourselves that we all feel to a greater or lesser degree.

Finding that axis and uniting the two (or two hundred, or two trillion) is what non-duality is all about. It comes back to body and soul. Body is to do with the physics, the structure, the biology, the science of our selves, the relationship that we sense we have with the world, with relativity, time and space; whereas soul, spirit, is another dimension altogether and one that can only be hinted at, alluded to and ultimately discoverable by each of us individually and personally, and accessed through awareness – and time. It is only through time that everything becomes channelled into our one journey.

MEMORIES, NOSTALGIA, THE PAST, LONGINGS, THE FUTURE

On thinking about the past, and how we can remember, but that we *can't* 'remember' the future, made me think that perhaps how we 'remember' the future is to do with semantics. The word 'remember' is what we call looking back, *nostalgia*, but looking forward is something to do with our imagination – even our fantasies and dreams, our hopes and ideas – and anticipation, which is similar to nostalgia. They are both a form of 'longing'. After all, we experience déjà vu and its cousin *jamais vu* (referring to the phenomenon of experiencing a situation that one somehow recognises although it seems very unfamiliar), and even sometimes *au futur vue* (view in the future – I confess I made this last one up, because I couldn't find a reference to having that sense of premonition). We are constantly living for a project of some sort. Projects tend towards the future, and that's what we do, we sort of imagine the future. We design the future, so we do have an idea – a longing – of what that projection will hold for us from our hopeful instigations. Sometimes we achieve our ambitions, ideas or projects, and sometimes we don't.

Later on, we look back and we think that perhaps we could have done things differently. Perhaps our anticipations and their outcomes are not vastly different from the past, because we consider either from the perspective of the present moment. It's partly a question of terminology. And sometimes, just as we might imagine the future one way and it comes out another, we remember events in our past differently. How do we really know what we remember correctly?

By increasing our practice of awareness, not randomly but genuinely and as continuously as possible, starting or increasing that awareness from this moment on, we will improve the quality of our memories which, in turn, will help us to shape our current and future experiences more accurately.

'I suspect that what we call the "flowing" of time has to be understood by studying the structure of our brain rather than by studying physics: evolution has shaped our brain into a machine that feeds off memory in order to anticipate the future...

'Our memories – which come from the past – hold together our sense of identity.'

The Order of Time,
CARLO ROVELLI

THE ORDER OF TIME

We need to be careful that we don't let our memories become distorted with the passage of time, which would then lead to a distorted sense of our identity. We should hold our memories lightly, allowing them to settle without colouring them in any way. We don't want to live in our memories, which would be lingering in the past, and we want our sense of self to flow effortlessly through the eternal present, being guided and shaped by events and circumstances as we live through them.

'Remembrance of things past is not necessarily the remembrance of things as they were.'

MARCEL PROUST

TIME HONOURED

We spend time trying to control not only everything that *we* do but also to a large extent other people's time and how they interact with us. There is a limit to how far the extent of our control can go. In recognising what those boundaries or limitations are we have to switch over to a certain degree of trust; trust that what we put in motion will unfold the best it can for us. Trust in letting go the things we can't control.

We will be a lot calmer if we can do this; we will be increasingly confident and with a better quality of time-spending. Our intuition, once given a direction, has a surprisingly good mechanism in place to manage our time, often more effectively than our brain/mind. The confidence in letting go and trusting our intuitive clock is akin to when we learned to ride a bike without stabilisers or to swim without floats. And it will free up a lot of stressful time *trying* to exercise control.

If in doubt, remember:
control = stress; trust = calm.

Another example of our intuitive timing is when we are on holiday or have a free day, at the weekend perhaps. When there are no commitments we seem to come up naturally with what we will do and what order we'll do things in – meeting up with friends, going out to buy coffee and newspapers to read leisurely, going for a swim – any number of non-committal activities seem to get channelled into a natural agenda. We can use this example for ourselves in order to have increased confidence in our inner time clock.

'*Time, like space, is a* **pure form of sense or intuition.**'

GEORG WILHELM FRIEDRICH HEGEL

ACCESSING YOUR INNER GUIDANCE

Everyone is born with an inner voice. In some people it's louder than for others, and it varies at different times in our lives. We can train ourselves to make space for this voice to be heard and to seek it out for that inner guidance. Take time to explore this, be in communication with it so that it isn't some random voice that we only occasionally experience. Through awareness and our own ways of practising mindfulness or meditation to bring the mind and body into coherent alignment, we can aim to connect to this infinite consciousness. The only currency it need cost you to unwrap this gift, is time.

Only by taking the time to exercise habitual practice can we make these connections and benefit from the knowledge gained and increase the fulfilment we seek in our lives.

We often complicate life choices by questioning and doubting our intuition, or being deaf to it through the chaos and stress we create. Learn to access, trust and apply your inner guidance.

'Time remains, to a large extent, a mystery, perhaps the greatest one. A mystery that relates to issues ranging from the fate of black holes to the enigma of our individual identity and consciousness...

'I also think we are beginning to see that we are time. We are this clearing opened by the traces of memory inside the connections between our neurons. We are memory. We are nostalgia. We are longing for a future that will not come.'

CARLO ROVELLI,
Author, director of quantum gravity research group at the centre of theoretical physics at Aix-Marseille University

Time is a great mystery, but let's make sense of how we personally relate to it, what it means to us and how we can, therefore, hold on to it and make the best use of it. By exploring the nature of time, we are led to discover something about ourselves, which, in turn, leads us back to understanding something about the nature of time. We are, therefore, in a continual and circular dance where we are both choreographer and dancer, composer and musician, the singer and the song.

*'Carpe diem, quam minimum
credula postero.'*

*(Pluck the day [for it is ripe], trusting as
little as possible in tomorrow.)*

The Odes of Horace,
HORACE

TIME IS STILL

Perhaps time doesn't move at all, maybe we move through it. As with space, which we move through, creating the relative sensation that time and space are moving. When you watch the sunset and you see the Sun go down, sinking below the horizon, it is not the Sun that is moving down but rather we on planet Earth, which is rotating in its orbit around the Sun. Rather like when you sit in a stationary train looking out at another stationary train that starts moving, and for a moment we think that it's our train that's on the move, and then for another moment we're not sure whether it's the other train or our train that's moving in an experience of relativity.

When we stay absolutely still, or sit in meditation, we become more at one with time itself, where we have the simpler sensation that neither time, nor we, move.

'Time is not a thing that passes ... it's a sea on which you float.'

ANONYMOUS

TIME ON YOUR HANDS

Have time on your side. It isn't against you. It isn't an enemy, although we often feel as though it is. A way to remember to do this and to achieve it is to link the association of it to your breath. When concentrating on your breath, you return to the breath as an anchor of awareness. You will gradually associate the breath with time, which is, in itself, a direct connection, because time and breathing are inextricably entwined.

THE PIVOTAL POINT IN DEVELOPMENT

We're at a moment in history where great change is taking place. When we go further into deep space in travel, then time travel, we will get used to the idea of having yet more different time zones. Or, we will become accustomed to the fact that as we travel in space we also travel in time: we are going to come back to Earth with a different age from the age we were when we left, and different again when compared to the people who have aged differently in the intervening years in Earth-time.

The pivotal point in development comes about because of the rapid development in technology, AI (artificial intelligence), in the need for (or the human thirst for) more and more accurately measured time. No matter how much we adjust to sophisticated clock mechanisms, in terms of the actual time we have to spend the time remains exactly the same.

THE RENAISSANCE ERA OF ARTIFICIAL INTELLIGENCE

On 10 February 1996, the chess-playing computer called Deep Blue, developed by IBM, surprised the world by defeating the chess grandmaster and reigning world champion Garry Kasparov in game one of a six-game match. AI had beaten the human mind.

All AI systems rely on being fed fuel. This is provided, simplistically, by everything we may have ever looked up, stored, socially mediated, shopped or emailed. Algorithms, which are instructions produced by computers by the data they're fed, were sophisticated short cuts to performance, for example, in predicting the success or failure on the financial market.

Perhaps initially the objective was to save time for the human operators to produce a better profit margin. But time at what cost? The genie is out of the AI bottle and it is set to continue influencing the future as definitively as the dawn of the renaissance era.

How we deal with this phenomenon is still up to us. Just.

PERCEPTIONS OF TIME

I asked several people to write something about their experience of time to give me a glimpse into other's perceptions. Here's what one friend wrote, thanks, Louis!

Wow, the more I think about it, the more I realise what a complex thing time is.

As I sit at Paddington station with 'time on my side', it makes me realise how it's the best thing in the world, or the worst.

When it's the best thing, it means that you are in control and you are beating it. You are not bound by it and the results of this mean that you are able to enjoy that moment, whether it be thinking (otherwise known as brain realignment), sleeping (brain realignment), or meditating (brain realignment)!

Does it suggest that 'positive time' is when you are not bound by it?

What would be negative time? I suppose that's when it's your enemy. It's there to work against you and mess up the brain realignment. You wish you could rewind it, have more of it.

Perhaps time is something that, if, as human beings, we could be in perfect harmony with, we would in fact glide through the little, or the long time, we have as intelligent human beings? Or perhaps that's the problem: we are not intelligent and have created an unnecessary thing to count down.

D
E
E
P

IT'S HARD TO BE COMPASSIONATE IF YOU'RE IN A HURRY

To be compassionate requires taking the time to focus and be aware of someone else's problems. The same applies with being a good listener, as this requires our full attention, not while scrolling for messages or writing an email, or even thinking about something else at the same time. Stop multi-tasking on important stuff.

'Listening itself is an art. When we listen with a still and concentrated mind it is possible to actually be responsive to what the words are saying.'

JOSEPH GOLDSTEIN

Pain and sorrow do not discriminate when we acknowledge other people's difficulties as well as their happiness and well-being. We all have essential ingredients, but most of all *we all share*, as long as we live, *one* commodity/asset that links us with every other human being on Earth – all 7.7 billion of us – and that is *time*.

'Love makes the time pass. Time makes love pass.'

EURIPIDES

MAKE A NOTE OR A CHART OF YOUR AVERAGE WEEK

Note down when you have natural highs and lows. Some people have a dip in the afternoon, whereas others do their best work in the morning or are notorious midnight-oil burners. Getting to know yourself this way will help you to work to your advantage by capitalising on your higher energy frequency and allow you to be able to compensate for your dips.

You could take a seven-minute power nap or practise mindfulness breathing at these times, or work out that carbs at lunchtime are making you sleepy in the afternoon and that these would be better in the evening when you might be winding down. Not only does our body experience highs and lows, but our spirit does too. Some people experience a sort of melancholy in the early evening when the day is ending or a joyful spark in the morning on waking up. Use these findings to improve your schedule by either compensating for, or benefiting from, your natural rhythms.

PROGRESSION OF LIFE AND CHANGE

Despite certain traits that we bring with us through life, there are many that change with time. The key thing to remember here is that we don't remain the same character throughout our lifetime. Over time we grow with changes, constantly flowing and reforming as we continue to evolve. This understanding reminds us to stop clinging on to what we *perceive* as our identity, and instead to increase our awareness of it growing and flowing.

In so doing we dispense identifying with an image of ourselves, our ego, that may be stuck for better or worse in a false or static sense of ourselves.

A SATISFYING LIFE

What is it to lead a good life? What is it to lead a satisfying and then ultimately a happy life?

When considering values of what is important to us in life and what qualities we need to strive towards, living an authentic life is the simplest and clearest quality we could attain in our quest to find the right life to lead and the right place to live it in. In order to consider – to really consider – this choice of an authentic life and what that means to each of us individually, we must make the time to contemplate the destination we want to reach.

'For what it's worth: it's never too late or, in my case, too early to be whoever you want to be. There's no time limit, stop whenever you want. You can change or stay the same, there are no rules to this thing. We can make the best or the worst of it. I hope you make the best of it. And I hope you see things that startle you. I hope you feel things you never felt before. I hope you meet people with a different point of view. I hope you live a life you're proud of. If you find that you're not, I hope you have the courage to start all over again.'

The Curious Case of Benjamin Button,
F. SCOTT FITZGERALD

CONSERVATION

There is a lot of discussion and emphasis on conservation – of wildlife, woodlands, the planet, the ocean, water – but less discussion about conservation of *time*. We need to pay attention to conservation of this vital asset and be aware of whether we are wasting our time and efforts. And if we think we are, then we need to identify where it is that we are wasting our time. On certain people? Too much unnecessary screen time? Too much time dwelling on regrets, or too much worry?

Make a spontaneous list and add anything that resonates here. This will quickly identify the areas where we can tighten up our time belt and have more quality time for other more fulfilling areas, or simply to have more *time in hand* for when we might need or want it.

This also serves to remind us how precious our time is. As we know: unless we regard something or someone as being precious, we will not value it.

FAST FASHION

The demand for ever newer, cheaper, more affordable, more accessible clothes and accessories in a throw-away-and-buy-again climate means that people in often terrible conditions are ill-paid for their time or are slaving to feed our demand. In a moment of reflection it is good to think about how we 'cost' other people's time in one way or another. Not just with respect to clothes but also to possessions, which are often far in excess of what we need, or even want, once we have them.

Whenever someone wastes our time, give a thought to whoever's time *we* have wasted, either consciously or unconsciously, directly or indirectly.

A mantra to bear in mind: love people and use things; not the other way around.

'You're only here for a short visit. Don't hurry, don't worry. And be sure to smell the flowers along the way.' This was the mantra of Sir Walter Hagen, the world's first full-time golf professional. Yet despite the schedule and demands on his career, he famously enjoyed his time both on and off the green.

However demanding your chosen profession is, and however challenging your business trips are, the above is a good reminder to schedule in something cultural to do when in new places, or to meet new people outside the work environment, to make the best use of your time.

'A person who has not done one half his day's work by ten o'clock, runs a chance of leaving the other half undone.'

Wuthering Heights,
EMILY BRONTË

MINDFULNESS NEWSMAN

An ABC news reporter, Dan Harris, on *Good Morning America* had a panic attack, on air, in front of five million viewers. He had burned out, spiralled out of control, living too fast a pace to suit his natural rhythm. And that breakdown on television was his changing point. He then took up meditation for the first time in his life. Initially, people were sceptical and even scornful, yet he persisted undeterred, and when asked why he was doing it, he said, 'Well it makes me 10 per cent happier – why wouldn't I?' He started to grip people's interest (after all who doesn't want to be 10 per cent happier?) and then their respect. Now he talks about constructive worry versus pointless rumination; and how much time we waste listening to the negative voices in our head telling us that we're not good enough.

You might worry, understandably, if the traffic is heavy and you're in danger of missing your flight, so you need to speed up a bit, but when you're in that journey and you've done everything you can to make it on time, but you find that circumstances outside your control are stacked against you, it's pointless ruminating beyond having done what you can.

The same with life generally: there is a certain amount of constructive worry that's useful, but then there's the worry, which manifests in ruminating and dwelling, that is absolutely not useful and a waste of time. It gets in the way of being connected to, and being grounded in, the present moment. We can learn something from these examples of other people's experiences. It can be helpful to put some of our own concerns or intentions into focus.

This is not to say that we can be meditating all the time or be mindful all the time, even if that is our aim, but it's a way of coming back to that essential reality and clarity and focus, which brings us back to the life authentic. When truth is the criterion, life rolls more smoothly.

Time consumption

The average person checks their phone or their emails 150 times a day, according to a study. When you've read this, you'll probably feel a strong urge to check your phone.

- A total of 78 per cent of all adults now own a smartphone.
- On average, people check them once every 12 minutes during their waking hours, the study claims.
- Two in five adults look at their phone within five minutes of waking, while a third check their phones just before falling asleep, according to the report.
- A high percentage (71 per cent) say that they never turn off their phone, and 78 per cent say they could not live without it.
- While three-quarters of the British public still regard voice calling as an important function of their phones, more (92 per cent) say Web browsing is crucial.

- Phone users in developed countries now spend about two hours a day on their little screens.

Is this better communication or simple time wasting?

MEDITATION FOR INSIGHT

For a cost-free, accessible practice, mindfulness and meditation are important parts of the structures of our lives in order to create space and time on a regular basis. Once we take the time to practise and hone mindfulness and meditation, after a while it's something that becomes embedded in our lives. We become mindful of other people's feelings and mindful of their situations, we become mindful of ourselves and mindful of our time expenditure. In other words, we are more aware.

We do this naturally, through habit and growth. We are living consciously instead of mindlessly. And meditation means seeking out that quiet space, both physically and then interiorly, and finding that quarter of an hour. Everyone has their own agenda, but just try it, whether it's 5, 10, 15 or 30 minutes. Find a time that works, because there are days when we are more fidgety or distracted than others, and they make it more difficult. Quite often, insights will come from meditation either immediately or after the mind has had time to access this quiet space.

Insights will come in whatever area you most need them. These insights are our pause buttons, our pauses in an otherwise hectic day.

**Not so much counting time as
making time count.**

BREATHING EXERCISE

To reduce your stress levels, do a breathing exercise daily.

Do it at times before a potentially stressful meeting or interview, or at any time when you need to circulate more oxygen to your brain to think more clearly and to remain calm.

1   Breathe in for the count of five seconds, then out for five seconds, for two minutes.
2   Be mindful, and focus only on your breathing during this time.

'Nothing in life is to be feared, it is only to be understood. Now is the time to understand more, so that we may fear less.'

MARIE CURIE

BE AWARE OF THE MOON, OR THE BIG CLOCK IN THE SKY

Paying attention to the Moon and becoming more aware of it on a daily basis will keep us tethered to time in the most natural way. Most diaries and calendars give the simplest of phases every month, so we know what to look out for if we miss some moons lost in cloudy nights. Tide tables and websites galore devote space to the phases of the Moon and the tide in detail. On a clear night, or a night with scuttling clouds, we can seek out the Moon and just be aware of it. Ponder on it a while – a nod to time. Look at the stars and know again how they were important factors for telling the time in primitive time-reckoning.

There is something primeval about seeing the full Moon every month – keeping in time with the biggest clock of them all – and the influence of the Moon on the powerful tides of the sea.

The same applies with the Sun, although we are more conscious of the Sun on a daily basis. There are times of the day – dawn, noon, dusk, sunset – when we might feel more in tune with the Sun and how it tells us its time, as we hurtle around it at a speed of about 18.5 miles (30km) per second.

Earth and the Sun are roughly 92.96 million miles (149.60 million km) apart, and one complete orbit takes 365.256 days, during which time Earth has travelled 584 million miles (940 million km).

All of which, considering the enormity of the universe and the tiny space we occupy within it, helps to put our lives into perspective.

FREEDOM FROM FEAR

Fear, a close relation to worry, is all about the future. Fear is anticipation of something inherently unpleasant that might, or equally might not, happen, because, as we know, anything in the future is in another 'time' zone. We also know from our own experience how many times we have worried about something in the future only to find that it didn't happen. And since that something might not transpire, we're worrying, or fearing something, unnecessarily. And you can't fear that same thing if or when it does transpire, because it is by then in the present. And you can't fear something that is in the present, I don't think, because once that very thing that you might have feared does transpire, and is upon you, you are no longer fearing 'it' because it is happening and you are dealing with 'it'.

Whatever it is and even if it is painfully difficult, you must deal with it in the now, so your mind and faculties are so occupied with handling it that there is not room for that same 'fear'. If you're still worrying about how the present predicament might eventually unfold, we're back to where we started: fearing something that might or might not happen in the future. Like the mother who sees that a horse has fallen on her child, there is no time for fear, as all her mind-power is directed into a superhuman strength that allows her to lift the horse up enough to free her child. If she remains on the sidelines worrying, then she is powerless and, by doing nothing, she is caught up in her own sense of fear.

Freedom from fear is a very real and very valid aspiration. Time spent thinking about this, and in some way helping us to succeed in our aspiration, will save us a huge amount of negative time worrying and fearing, as well as giving us freedom from that low-level fear that lurks. Even when there is nothing specific to fear, the darker side of our brain will be out there on the lookout if it is given half a chance. This freedom gives us room to enjoy other more real and positive events or adventures.

If the opposite of freedom is imprisonment,
and imprisonment is a curtailing of our time,
then freedom = time.

'We are endowed with a body... it has a sense of the rhythm of life and a sense of time, not only of hours and days, but also of decades; the body regulates its own childhood, puberty and maturity, stops growing when it should no longer grow, and brings forth a wisdom tooth at a time when no one of us ever thought of it.'

The Importance of Living,
LIN YUTANG

Here is a difficult hurdle: the freedom that comes from ultimately conquering the big fear – the fear of death – when our time literally runs out.

This is not some idle thought dressed up to soften anything or to offer freedom from death itself, but freedom from the *fear* of death.

*'Death is neither depressing nor exciting; it
is simply a fact of life'*

SOGYAL RINPOCHE

It is very important to spend time on this, and it might need great fortitude in conquering it, but by opening ourselves up to it is, in itself, a way of diluting that fear. No one has come back to tell us how it is to die, no one has come back to say what it's like on the other side, so this is the starting point.

How do we know that, actually, the end of life might be manageable on some level or another – on a level that we aren't yet equipped to understand because that manageability is only given when it is needed. Just as the mother's superhuman strength was given to her when, and only when, she needed it. What are our fears? Fear of losing our loved ones, fear of ill health, fear of loss of some sort, and the fear of mortality?

If we can come to terms with the inevitability of our eventual death and can release ourselves from the fear that that knowledge brings, then we have conquered fear itself and we have the joy of freedom in our lives. If fear is all about anticipating something in the future, including our death, really it is the fear of the unknown that we are talking about, as we have no idea what the circumstances of our passing will be. Ideally, we need to remove fear in our lives at a point before our death, as, after all, none of us know when our 'time' is up, so let's not waste what we have by anticipating it.

Who knows, perhaps it has, at that final moment, an unexpected glory about it – an unimaginable 'lightness of being' to quote Milan Kundera, or even a joyfulness in that release. I remember when Bobby, my mum, was dying she squeezed my hand and said with sudden alacrity, 'there is nothing to fear', and she had an extraordinarily peaceful smile on her face. I think she really believed that, she lived that, and at the end died with that.

There are many books and much in the way of enlightened talks and legacies on the subject, by teachers, writers and aspirants far better equipped than I am, to take you further on this particular journey. But it is discussed here as a vital part of our meditation and the key to our freedom in life, our freedom from fear. And the freedom in our minds from time spent constantly worrying about future time.

'That said, the basic idea of Being and Time is extremely simple: being is time. That is, what it means for a human being to be is to exist temporally in the stretch between birth and death.'

MARTIN HEIDEGGER

'All we have to decide is what to do with
the time that is given us.'

The Fellowship of the Ring,
J.R.R. TOLKIEN

TRANSITION

Janus was the god of time, of beginnings and transitions in Roman mythology. He was depicted as having two faces looking in opposite directions, one towards the past and the other towards the future. He presided over passages, doorways and gates, and over transitions between youth and old age, growth and decay, war and peace.

We are all in a constant state of transition of one sort or another. The key is to know who we are and where we are as we transition: job, gender, relationship, age, past to present to future.

In order to go with the flow joyfully through all our transitions, I believe that the more we can be aware of the value of our time the more we will succeed. Perhaps the biggest transition is the one we have to make between our own natural time and the unnatural time frame in which we constantly try to slot ourselves. Instead of constantly feeling the pull *between* the two, let's find instead the best balance of both that we can.

'It all comes down to time in the end. The young they want to get older, the old they want to get younger. Somewhere in the middle, at the halfway mark, here I am, Janus-like, facing forwards while looking back. Janus, the god of gateways and goodbyes, transitions and new beginnings.'

How Hard Can it Be?,
ALLISON PEARSON

We have come full circle from where we began: Bang or no Bang. For if there was a beginning to time, then it implies that there will be an end. If, on the other hand, your theory is that there was no beginning, then, conversely, there will be no end to time.

And who knows what will happen between here and the rest of eternity?

Only time will tell.

ACKNOWLEDGEMENTS

A huge thank you to my agent, Jane Turnbull, for her support and guidance, and to Jillian Young, my editor at Little, Brown for her patience and perspicacity. Thanks also to the late, great film publicist Theo Cowan, for innumerable long lunches in London and Cannes (he was known as a legend in his own lunchtime) back in the 1980s, when we would incessantly discuss our mutual love of the subject time. I'd like to acknowledge the teaching of philosophers (Eastern and Western) and followers of Tao for their guidance and knowledge over the years, as well as contemporary ones for allowing me to include extracts or quotations from their own work. I am grateful to Vince Gaffney for his contribution on primitive timekeeping; to physicists Carlo Rovelli and Paul Davies, who were very generous in allowing me to refer to material in their own books *The Order of Time* and *About Time*, respectively. And a big thank you to close friends and family for their contributions and encouragement.